Basic Statistics Using Excel for Office XP

for use with

Statistical Techniques in Business & Economics

Twelfth Edition

Douglas A. Lind
Coastal Carolina University

William G. Marchal
University of Toledo

Samuel A. Wathen
Coastal Carolina University
Wall College of Business

Supplement Prepared by
Ronald Merchant
University of Phoenix

Renee Goffinet
and
Virginia Koehler
Spokane Falls Community College

 **McGraw-Hill**
Irwin

Boston   Burr Ridge, IL   Dubuque, IA   Madison, WI   New York   San Francisco   St. Louis
Bangkok   Bogotá   Caracas   Kuala Lumpur   Lisbon   London   Madrid   Mexico City
Milan   Montreal   New Delhi   Santiago   Seoul   Singapore   Sydney   Taipei   Toronto

Basic Statistics Using Excel for Office XP for use with
STATISTICAL TECHNIQUES IN BUSINESS & ECONOMICS
Douglas A. Lind, William G. Marchal and Samuel A. Wathen

1 2 3 4 5 6 7 8 9 0 QPD/QPD 0 9 8 7 6 5 4

ISBN 0-07-286828-7

www.mhhe.com

The McGraw-Hill Companies

McGRAW-HILL/Irwin

Basic Statistics Using Excel for Office XP for use with STATISTICAL TECHNIQUES IN BUSINESS & ECONOMICS, Twelfth Edition by Lind, Marchal and Wathen.

We hope this manual and the text are error free and easy for you to use. Invariably, however, if there are errors, we would appreciate knowing about such errors as soon as possible so that we can correct them in subsequent printings and future editions. Please help us by using this postage-paid form to report any that you find. Thank you.

Note: Extra copies of this form appear at the end of this manual.
Attention: R. T. Hercher

Name _____   School _____

Office Phone _____

Please fold and seal so that our address is visible.

BUSINESS REPLY MAIL
FIRST-CLASS MAIL   PERMIT NO.204   OAKBROOK, IL

POSTAGE WILL BE PAID BY ADDRESSEE

ATTENTION: R. T. Hercher

THE McGRAW-HILL COMPANIES
1333 BURR RIDGE PKY.
BURR RIDGE, IL 60527-0085

(fold)

(fold)

PREFACE

Basic Statistics Using Excel for Office XP is a workbook, which empowers students to use the computer to help them understand and apply the basic tools taught in an introductory statistics course. When students use Excel to experiment and illustrate their problems, they can better visualize them and more easily see what happens.

Given the popularity of Excel and its expanded capacity to handle statistical data, it is a natural in colleges; in fact, many colleges have Excel on all of their computers. In addition, Excel is the software of choice in today's business world. What students learn with Excel can often be applied immediately on the job as well as in other classes. Many students have been exposed to this powerful software program and may already have it on their own computers.

This workbook is especially designed to accompany the Twelfth Edition of **Statistical Techniques in Business and Economics** by Douglas A. Lind, William G. Marchal, and Samuel A. Wathen. It also works well with the Fourth Edition of **Basic Statistics for Business and Economics** by Lind, Marchal, and Wathen. Both of these books tend to use Excel on problems where the authors feel Excel is superior and Minitab where they feel Minitab is superior. **This workbook fills a special niche for instructors who use only Excel in their courses**. It can also be used as a companion to most other introductory statistics texts, or by itself.

The chapter goals listed at the beginning of each chapter provides overviews of the main topics covered and the tasks students should be able to do after having worked through the chapter.

Following each chapter are several exercises to provide additional practice in applying the topics covered. Thus the students can check their comprehension of the material as they progress through each chapter. These exercises can also be used as class assignments.

The illustrations in this workbook are from Excel 2002, more commonly known as Excel XP; however, the material has been used successfully with previous versions of Excel. Excel XP is fully backwards compatible with Excel 2000. This means that you can open, edit, and save files between both versions (XP and 2000), without having to save them as a previous version.

If you are using Excel 2003, you should not have any problems using this workbook.

Ronald Merchant
Renee C. Goffinet
Virginia E. Koehler

ACKNOWLEDGMENTS

We are grateful to many people for the help and encouragement throughout the development of this workbook: Mike Antonucci, Gail Korosa and Christina Sanders at McGraw-Hill Irwin, our students for their patience while classroom testing our rough drafts, and the feedback from several reviewers. Julie Sanborn's editing skills improved the earlier versions of this manuscript immensely.

We welcome comments about the book and suggestions for improvement:

Ron Merchant
4501 East Walnut Road
Gilbert, AZ 85297

rmerch@qwest.net

CONTENTS

CHAPTER

1

USING MICROSOFT EXCEL SPREADSHEETS

CHAPTER GOALS

After completing this chapter, you will be able to:

1. Understand why Excel is so useful as a statistical tool.

2. Define what is meant by a spreadsheet.

3. Enter data into a spreadsheet.

4. Create formulas and solve problems with a worksheet.

5. Edit data that is in a spreadsheet.

6. Use a spreadsheet to experiment and illustrate.

Introduction

Welcome to **Basic Statistics Using Excel**.

Excel is the most popular spreadsheet program in the world and has the capacity to handle a wide variety of statistical applications. Most colleges have Excel on their campus computers; it is part of the Microsoft Office package. You may have already had some exposure to Excel and used it for other applications. You may even have Excel on your home computer.

Using Excel will enhance your ability to understand and apply statistical principles. It is the software choice in the business world.

Basically, spreadsheets are used to help you with analysis of numerical data and to solve problems. In a spreadsheet, you can enter data that is related, and see what the results are if you change that data. You can create charts and graphs. You can run statistical analysis. Spreadsheets are used in businesses by managers to assist in decision making.

This chapter is for those who have never used a spreadsheet or worksheet, or for those who want a review of the basics.

Open Microsoft Excel. You may need to ask how the system you are using operates. A task pane opens on the right side of the worksheet window, providing you with document options: Open a workbook, New from existing workbook, and New from template. You may close the task pane to provide more workspace on your screen by selecting View, Task Pane from the Menu bar.

The first row of your Microsoft Excel worksheet is called the Menu bar. The second and third rows are called Tool bars. You will often be requested to select a button from either the Menu bar or the Tool bar.

As your mouse pointer rests on each button of the Tool bar, a short description is displayed just below that button.

Creating a New Worksheet

If a blank worksheet does not appear, you will need to create a new worksheet.

To create a new worksheet select File, from the Menu bar. Select New. Or you may select the button for a new page.

The worksheet consists of rows, columns and cells. Each individual rectangle is a *cell*. Each cell is identified by it placement in the Column (A, B, C ...) and the Row (1, 2, 3 ...). Thus, the cell B3 would be in the 2nd column and the 3rd row. The mouse pointer in Excel looks like an open plus sign. When the pointer is on a cell, click the left mouse button and that cell becomes the active cell. The cell will have a dark bordered box around it. You can also use the arrow keys: up, down, right, left, to move around in the worksheet.

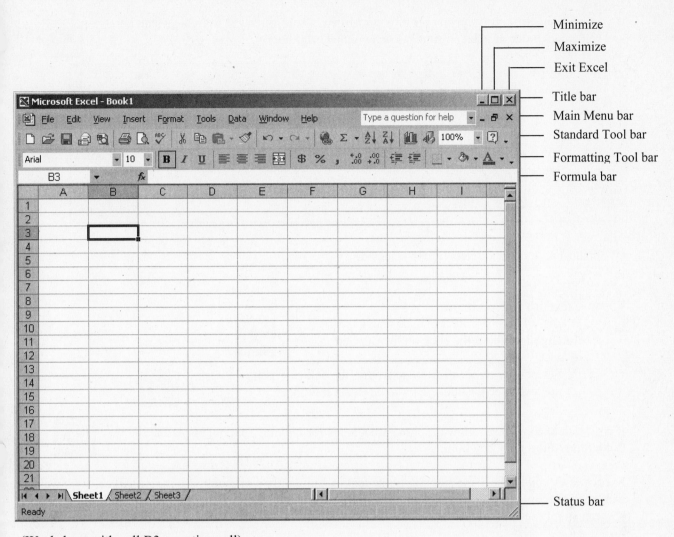

Minimize
Maximize
Exit Excel
Title bar
Main Menu bar
Standard Tool bar
Formatting Tool bar
Formula bar
Status bar

(Worksheet with cell B3 as active cell)

The data or information you key will show in the active cell and in the formula bar. When you press the <Enter> key, your data is entered into the cell and the cell immediately below becomes the active cell. Or you can point to another cell or use your arrow keys. To edit a cell, double click your mouse pointer in that cell, and the cell can be edited. The mouse pointer will show as a large I instead of an open plus. You may then edit the cell, without rekeying the entire contents.

You can select several cells at once to work with, called a range. A *range* is a rectangular group of cells. To use your mouse, you would place your mouse pointer on the upper left cell of the range to be highlighted, then click, hold and drag your mouse pointer to the lower right cell of the range, and then release the mouse button. The first cell shows a white background, all other cells in the selected range show a black background. A range is identified by its first and last cells with a colon in between.

1. Activate cell A1 by clicking on it, key **Schools** and press <Enter>.

2. Cell A2 should now be active. Key **Roads**. Key in the remaining data so that your worksheet looks like the one on the next page. Use the incorrect spelling of Supplie in cell A4.

If you make an error, you can correct it by immediately selecting Edit from the Menu bar, and selecting Undo, or you can simply click on the Undo button.

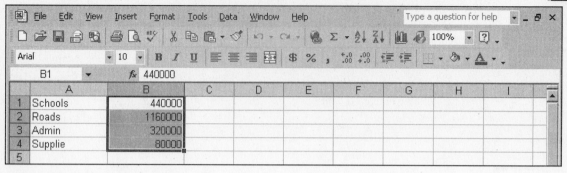

(Worksheet with range of cells B1:B4 selected)

To move text to a new position

1. Highlight the cells, click on the Cut button.

2. Select the new location by activating the cell in which you wish the text to be located, click on the Paste button.

If you wish to copy text, follow the same procedures for moving text, but instead of the Cut button, select the Copy button.

Excel allows you to check the spelling of the text in your entire workbook or just selected cells. However, worksheets are often created using abbreviations which this feature may not recognize. If this happens you can simply select Ignore.

1. To check the spelling of the whole workbook simply click on the Spelling   button. A dialogue box will appear.

Depending on the cell that is active when you select the Spelling button, you may receive the following dialogue box. If you have not checked for spelling yet, then select Yes.

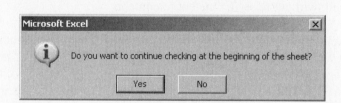

2. Click on Supplies and select Change. Select OK.

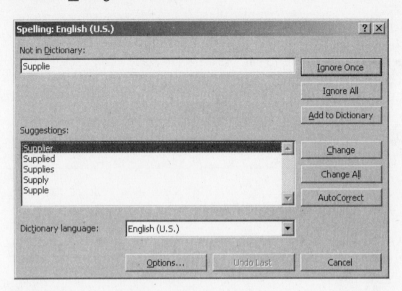

To check a selected area, highlight the cell or cells you want Excel to check, click on the Spelling button, and follow the same procedure as above.

You may create your worksheet in either portrait or landscape orientation by doing the following:

1. From the Menu bar, select File. Select Page Setup. A dialogue box appears with four tabs.

2. The Page tab should already be selected. You may select the radio button for Portrait or Landscape. Select OK.

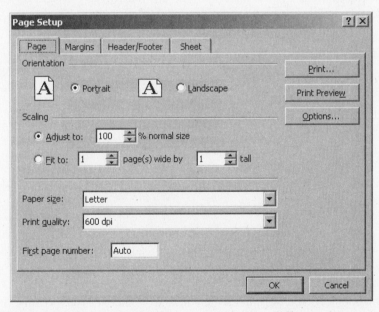

NOTE: As you work through this text, some illustrations may appear different than your screen.

Saving a Worksheet

To save a worksheet (file) do the following:

1. Select <u>F</u>ile, from the Menu bar. Select Save <u>A</u>s.

2. Key in the desired file name in the File <u>n</u>ame text box, key **Tax Dollars**.

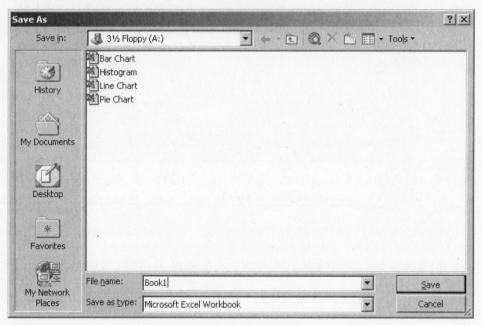

3. At the top of the dialog box, click on the down arrow at the right of the Save <u>i</u>n: text box. Click your mouse on 3 ½ Floppy (A:).

4. Click on <u>S</u>ave.

Closing a Worksheet

To close a worksheet (file) do the following:

1. Select <u>F</u>ile, from the Menu bar. Select <u>C</u>lose.

2. If no changes have been made since the last save, the file will close and the screen will be blank.

3. If the current information has not been saved you may select <u>Y</u>es to save the changes, select <u>N</u>o if you do not want to save the changes, or select Cancel to go back to the current worksheet.

After you close a worksheet, you need to create a new worksheet or retrieve an existing worksheet to continue working.

Retrieving a Worksheet

1. Select <u>F</u>ile from the Menu bar. Select <u>O</u>pen.

You may also open an existing document by selecting the **Open icon** on the **Tool bar**.

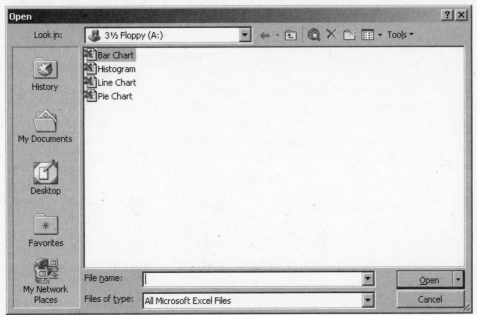

2. Verify the location of the file you wish to retrieve. You may have to change the selection in the **Look in:** text box at the top of the active window. The arrow to the right of the text box will allow you to access a pull down list of file location options.

3. Highlight the file that you wish to retrieve by placing your mouse curser over the file name and click the left mouse button once.

If you do not see your file located in this folder, try selecting **All Files** from the **Files of** <u>t</u>**ype:** drop down list at the bottom of the dialogue box.

4. Once the file is highlighted, select <u>O</u>pen.

5. After making any changes, save and close the worksheet.

Using Excel to Solve Problems

Use a new worksheet to create formulas and solve problems. The following problem is an example of how one can use the worksheet.

We are interested in finding the percentage of change in the U.S. Department of Labor's projections of Fast-Growing Occupations in the United States from 2000 to 2010.

	Employment	
Occupation	2000	2010
Computer support specialists	506,000	996,000
Computer system analysts	431,000	689,000
Personal home-care aids	414,000	672,000
Computer software engineers	389,000	760,000
Medical assistants	329,000	516,000
Dental assistants	234,000	320,000
Social service assistants	271,000	418,000
Fitness/aerobics trainers	158,000	222,000
Medical records technicians	136,000	202,000
Database administrators	106,000	176,000

Source: U.S. Department of Labor

NOTE: As you enter information on the Excel worksheet, start **all** formulas with an = sign to distinguish a formula from text.

To enter this problem on your new worksheet, do the following.

1. Key the heading, **Occupation** in cell A1.

2. In cells A2 to A11, key in the occupations.

3. In cell A12, key in the word **Total**.

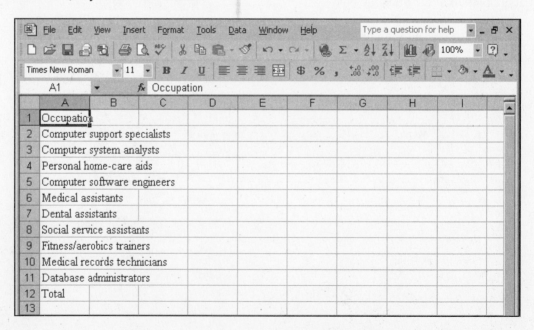

4. Notice that the names of the occupations extend into column B. To widen and automatically fit the column width, place the mouse pointer in the column headings row between columns A and B. The mouse pointer changes to a thick, black plus sign. Double click the left mouse button. The column automatically widens.

5. Key **2000** in cell B1 and **2010** in cell C1.

6. Fill in the amounts for 2000 in cells B2 to B11 and the amounts for 2010 in cells C2 to 11. Do not enter the commas as you enter the amounts.

7. There are a couple of different ways to sum several cells. Make cell B12 the active cell. Key **=sum(b2:b11)**. Touch the <Enter> key. The sum of the cells now shows in cell B12.

8. Now highlight cells, C2 to C11. To do so, put your mouse arrow on cell C2, click and drag down to cell C11. From the Tool bar, click on the AutoSum function button. Excel automatically enters the sum of the highlighted cells immediately below.

9. In cell D1 key **% change**.

10. Make cell D2 the active cell. Key the formula **=(c2-b2)/b2**. Touch the <Enter> key. The percent of change shows as a decimal number.

11. Make cell D2 the active cell. Put your mouse pointer on the lower right corner of the cell. It will show a small black box called a handle. The mouse pointer on the handle will show as a thick, black plus. Click your mouse button, hold and drag the mouse pointer down to cell D11.

Cells D3 to D11 have automatically been filled in with the formula.

	A	B	C	D	E
1	Occupation	2000	2010	% change	
2	Computer support specialists	506000	996000	0.968379	
3	Computer system analysts	431000	689000	0.598608	
4	Personal home-care aids	414000	672000	0.623188	
5	Computer software engineers	389000	760000	0.953728	
6	Medical assistants	329000	516000	0.568389	
7	Dental assistants	234000	320000	0.367521	
8	Social service assistants	271000	418000	0.542435	
9	Fitness/aerobics trainers	158000	222000	0.405063	
10	Medical records technicians	136000	202000	0.485294	
11	Database administrators	106000	176000	0.660377	
12	Total	2974000	4971000		

12. Highlight cells D2 to D11. From the Menu bar select Format. Select Cells. The Number tab should already be selected. Under the Category list box, select Percentage. In the Decimal places text box key **0** or click on the down arrow to display **0**. Click on OK. The amounts in column D now show as percentages instead of decimals.

Sometimes you want to rearrange the columns. If you want to show a graph of the percents of change use columns A and D. To move the column D (% change) next to the column A (Country), do the following.

13. Click your mouse pointer anywhere in column B.

14. From the **Menu bar,** select **I**nsert. Select **Columns.**

The information in columns B through D have been shifted to the right creating a blank column, with the width of column A.

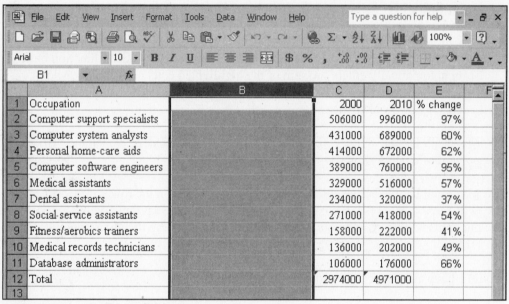

15. Highlight cells **E1 to E11**.

16. From the **Menu bar,** select **E**dit. Select **Cut**.

17. Make cell B1 your active cell. From the **Menu bar** select **E**dit. Select **P**aste.
    The columns with % change are now next to the column Country. You may also use the cut and paste icons on your tool bar.

	A	B	C	D	E
1	Occupation	% change	2000	2010	
2	Computer support specialists	97%	506000	996000	
3	Computer system analysts	60%	431000	689000	
4	Personal home-care aids	62%	414000	672000	
5	Computer software engineers	95%	389000	760000	
6	Medical assistants	57%	329000	516000	
7	Dental assistants	37%	234000	320000	
8	Social service assistants	54%	271000	418000	
9	Fitness/aerobics trainers	41%	158000	222000	
10	Medical records technicians	49%	136000	202000	
11	Database administrators	66%	106000	176000	
12	Total		2974000	4971000	

18. On the thick black plus sign between the column headings B and C, double click the left mouse button to resize the column width of B.

	A	B	C	D	E
1	Occupation	% change	2000	2010	
2	Computer support specialists	97%	506000	996000	
3	Computer system analysts	60%	431000	689000	
4	Personal home-care aids	62%	414000	672000	
5	Computer software engineers	95%	389000	760000	
6	Medical assistants	57%	329000	516000	
7	Dental assistants	37%	234000	320000	
8	Social service assistants	54%	271000	418000	
9	Fitness/aerobics trainers	41%	158000	222000	
10	Medical records technicians	49%	136000	202000	
11	Database administrators	66%	106000	176000	
12	Total		2974000	4971000	
13					

You can also select non-adjacent columns, simply highlight one of the columns, hold down the <Ctrl> key while highlighting another column. This can be done with as many as you wish.

Save your worksheet if you wish. Close your worksheet.

Exiting Excel

Select File from the Menu bar. Select Exit. This ends your Excel session.

CHAPTER

2

DESCRIBING DATA: FREQUENCY DISTRIBUTIONS AND GRAPHIC PRESENTATIONS

CHAPTER GOALS

After completing this chapter, you will be able to:

1. Use Excel to create such common graphic presentations as pie charts, bar charts, simple histograms and line charts.

2. Edit and modify charts.

3. Print charts to be used alone or embedded in a report.

Introduction

The graphic presentations you see extensively in newspapers including *USA Today*, magazines and governmental reports often portray data from a frequency distribution in the form of pie charts, bar charts, histograms and line charts. Chapter 2 shows you how you can use Excel to create these charts and graphs.

Microsoft Excel's worksheets calculate and present differences and similarities between numbers, and changes in numbers over time. While these worksheets are useful they are often cumbersome to read. When you *illustrate* the data graphically it is often easier for your message to be understood. Sometimes a picture is worth a thousand words. With charts, you can make your data visual. You can create a chart to show the changes in your data over time, or how the parts of your data fit together as a whole. You can rearrange your data, even after you have charted it, or added additional data. With Microsoft Excel and ChartWizard, you can easily turn your data into dynamic graphic presentations.

Pie charts show the relationship of parts to a whole. Bar charts show comparison between items or comparison over time. Line charts are often best for showing the amount of change in values over time. As you use different types of graphic presentations you will get to know which chart is best for your data. Since it is so easy you may want to experiment with several types of charts to see which chart does the best job of clarifying your point.

To create a chart on a worksheet, you will select the data that you want to use in the chart, and then click the *ChartWizard* button on the Tool bar. The following exercises will take you step by step though the creation of several charts.

Pie Charts and Bar Charts

Example 1. The Clayton County Commissioners want to design a chart to show the taxpayers attending the forthcoming meeting what happens to their tax dollars. The total amount of taxes collected is $2 million. Expenditures were: $440,000 for schools, $1,160,000 for roads, $320,000 for administration, and $80,000 for supplies.

The instructions for entering the data and creating a pie chart are as follows:

If you saved the data Tax Dollars in Chapter 1, open the file and proceed with step 3. Otherwise do the following.

1. On a new worksheet, enter in cells A1:A4, the expenditure headings: **Schools, Roads, Admin** and **Supplies**.

NOTE: It is very important that all headings fit in **one** column. Either abbreviate the headings or widen the column to accommodate the length of the widest one.

2. Enter in cells B1:B4, the expenditure amounts: **440000, 1160000, 320000** and **80000**.

3. Position the mouse on cell A1, hold the left mouse button and drag until cells A1:B4 are highlighted.

As mentioned in Chapter 1, the first cell shows a white background and all other cells in the selected range show a black background.

4. From the Tool bar click on the ChartWizard icon.

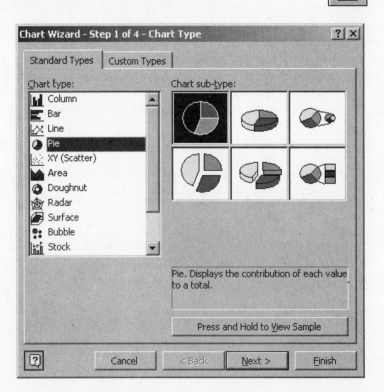

5. Chart Wizard Steps 1 – 4 will appear in sequence. In step 1, the Standard Types tab should already be selected. Under Chart type, click on Pie.

6. Several Chart sub-types are displayed. Choose the 1ˢᵗ one in the upper left corner. Click Next.

7. In step 2, the Data Range tab should already be selected. The Data range text box should display =**Sheet1!$A$1:$B$4**. Series in Columns should already be selected.

If you select the Series tab you get a dialog box that shows the range of the selected Values and Category Labels. You could enter a chart title in the Name text box, but for now click Next.

8. In step 3 select the Titles tab if needed. In the Chart title text box, key **Tax Dollar Expenditures**. Click on the Legend tab. The check box for Show legend may be checked. Click on the box to de-select Show legend. Click on the Data Labels tab. Check the boxes for Category name and Percentage. Click Next.

9. In step 4 you can save the sheet as a new worksheet or as an object in the current worksheet. As object in Sheet 1 should be selected. Click Finish. A pie chart is formed with the percents and labels shown.

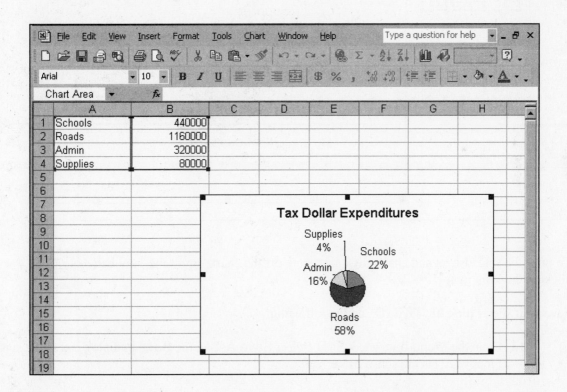

A box appears around the chart. A small box, called a *handle*, shows at each corner and in the middle of each line. To make your chart larger and easier to read, do the following.

10. Click and hold the left mouse button inside the chart. A 4-way arrow will show in the chart. As you move the chart it will show as an open box with dashed lines.

11. With your mouse button still depressed, move your chart so the left side is just to the right of column B and the top is in row 1.

12. Put your mouse arrow on the handle in the middle of the bottom line. You should have a horizontal line with an arrow on both ends.

13. Click the mouse, hold down and drag to row 16.

The chart is now larger and easier to read.

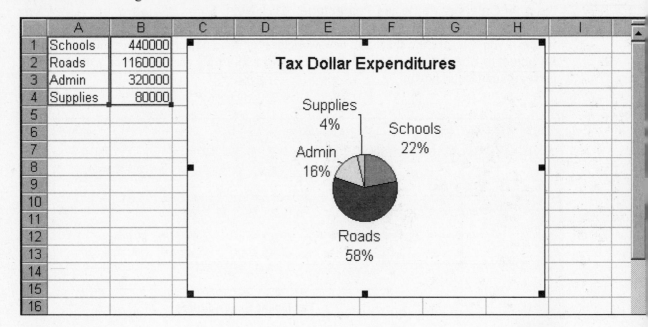

To print the spreadsheet and chart, click anywhere off the chart. From the Tool bar, click on the Print icon.

Save your file as **pie-cht**. To do so, do the following:

14. From the Menu bar, select File. Select Save As. In the Save in dialog box make sure 3 ½ Floppy (A:) is the active drive.

If 3 ½ Floppy (A:) is not active, click on the down arrow at the right of the Save in: text box. Click your mouse on 3 ½ Floppy (A:).

15. Once 3 ½ Floppy (A:) is active, click on the File name text box and key **pie-cht** in the text box. You may need to delete the existing name. Click Save.

Example 2. Do the following to change the chart to a horizontal bar chart:

1. Click your mouse anywhere inside the chart. The handles will show on the box. Click the **right** mouse button. A text box will appear.

2. Select Chart Type. Select Bar. Under Chart sub-type, the 1st chart in the upper left corner should be selected. Click OK.

3. Point your mouse arrow between two of the bars. A pull down box should show reading Plot Area. Click your **right** mouse button. Select Chart Options. At the top, select the Data Labels Tab. Value should be selected. Deselect Category name.. Click OK.

The data now shows as a horizontal bar chart.

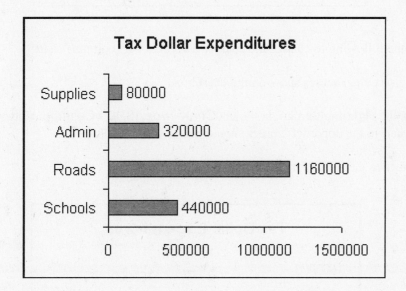

To print just the chart, make sure the handles show on the chart box. Click on the Print icon. If the handles do *not* show on the chart box, *both* the spreadsheet and chart will print.

To display the expenditures in reverse order, do the following:

4. Make sure the handles show on the chart box.

5. Click your mouse arrow on the **vertical y-axis** of the graph. It will have a box on the top and bottom of the line.

6. Click on your **right** mouse button. Choose Format Axis. At the top, select the Scale tab. At the bottom of the screen, select the check box for Categories in reverse order. Select Value (Y) axis Crosses at maximum category. (The bottom three lines will all have a check mark in the box.) Click OK.

The expenditures are now reversed.

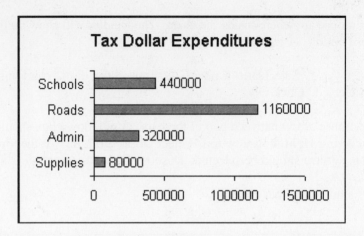

Example 3. Do the following to change the chart to a vertical bar (column) chart:

1. Make sure the handles show on the chart box.

2. Click the **right** mouse button. Select Chart Type. Select Column. Under Chart sub-type, the chart in the upper left corner should be selected. Click OK.

The data now shows in the form of a vertical bar (column) chart.

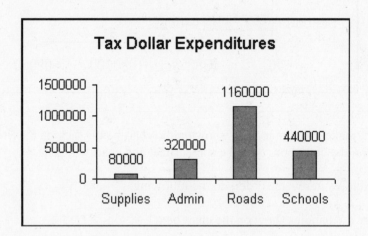

If you wish, save your file as **chart-1**. Close your file.

Simple Histograms

Example 4. The annual imports of a selected group of electronic suppliers are shown in the following frequency distributions.

Imports ($millions)	Number of suppliers
$ 2 up to $5	6
5 up to 8	13
8 up to 11	20
11 up to 14	10
14 up to 17	1

Portray the imports in the form of a histogram.

1. First determine the midpoint of each range in the import column, then use that midpoint for the x-axis data. This is given to you below.

2. On a new worksheet, enter the data as shown below.

	A	B	C	D	E	F	G	H	I
1	Imports	Suppliers							
2	3.5	6							
3	6.5	13							
4	9.5	20							
5	12.5	10							
6	15.5	1							
7									

3. With your mouse arrow on A1, click and drag to highlight **A1:B6**.

4. From the Tool bar, select ChartWizard.

5. In Step 1, under Chart type, select Column. Under Chart sub-type, the upper left chart should be selected. Click Next.

6. In Step 2, at the top, select the Series tab. Under the Series list box, **Imports** should be highlighted. Select Remove. (We don't want the Imports as part of the values). At the bottom, in the Category (X) axis labels text box, click on the icon at the far right.

Put your cursor on cell A2, click, hold and drag to cell A6. There will be a running box around cells **A2:A6**. Touch <Enter>. This identifies the first column as the x-axis labels. Click Next.

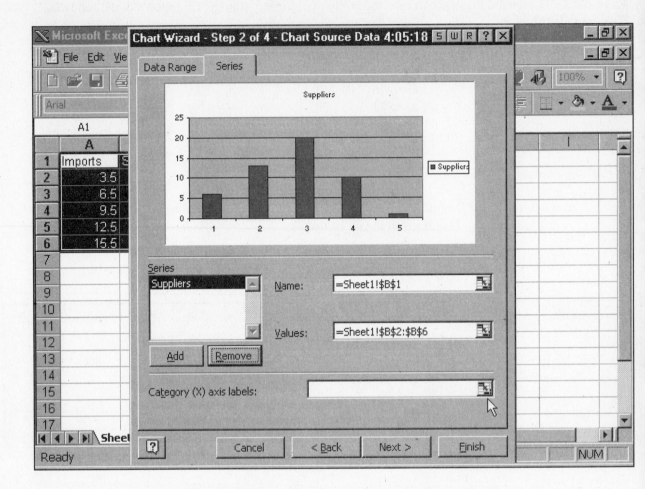

7. In Step 3, at the top, the Titles tab should be selected. Click on the Chart title text box, key **Annual Imports of Electronic Suppliers**. Tab to the Category (X) axis text box. Key **Annual Imports ($millions)**. Tab to the Value (Y) axis text box. Key **Number of Suppliers**.

8. At the top, select the Legend tab. Click in the Show legend check box to de-select the legend. Click Finish.

A condensed chart is shown.

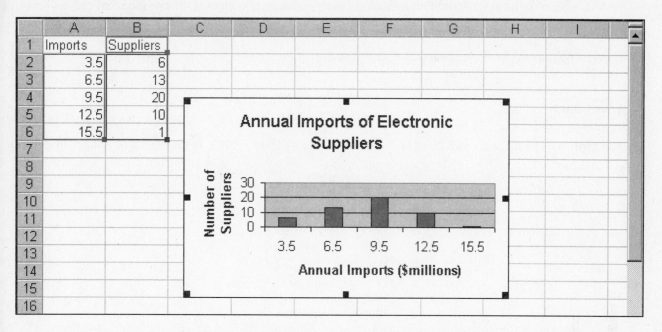

To make your chart larger, click on the middle handle of the top line and drag the line to row 1.

9. Make sure the handles show on the chart box. With your **right** mouse arrow, click on one of the columns. Select F_ormat Data Series.

10. At the top select the Options tab. In the Gap _width text box, click on the down arrow until the Gap _width reads 0. Click OK.

This displays your chart in the form of a histogram.

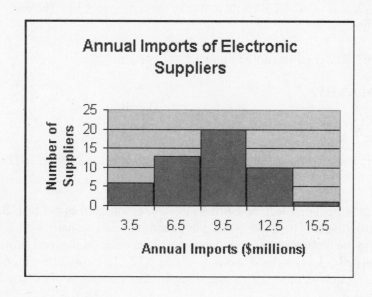

As shown you can use a column chart to create a simple histogram. Excel has a histogram analysis tool to determine a frequency distribution table and prepare a histogram chart from raw data, but that will not be included in this introductory chapter on charts.

If you wish, save your file as **chart-2**. Close your file.

Line Charts

Example 5. The net sales of Klassy Fashions for the years 1994 – 2003, in thousands of dollars, are:

	Net sales
Year	(in thous.)
1994	123.4
1995	144.1
1996	201.9
1997	232.4
1998	311.2
1999	410.8
2000	466.9
2001	512.7
2002	552.8
2003	557.6

To visual the data as a line chart, do the following:

1. On a new worksheet, key **Year** in cell A2, **Net Sales** in B1 and **in thous** in B2. Key **1994** and **1995** in cells A3:A4.

2. Highlight **A3:A4.** Place your cursor on the lower right box. The cursor will change to a thick black plus sign. Click, hold and drag the cursor to A12. The rest of the dates are automatically filled in.

3. In cells B3:B12 enter the dollar amounts.

4. Highlight **A3:B12**.

5. Select ChartWizard from the Tool bar.

6. In Step 1, under Chart type, select Line. Under Chart sub-type, select the 1st upper left chart. Click Next.

7. In Step 2, at the top, select the Series tab. Under the Series list box, **Series1** should be highlighted. Select Remove. (We don't want the years as part of the values). At the bottom, in the Category (X) axis labels text box, click on the icon at the far right. Put your cursor on cell A3, click, hold and drag to cell A12. There will be a running box around cells **A3:A12**. Touch <Enter>. This identifies the first column as the x-axis labels. Click Next.

8. In Step 3, at the top, the Titles tab should be selected. Click on the Chart title text box, key **Klassy Fashions Net Sales**. Tab to the Category (X) axis text box. Key **Years**. Tab to the Value (Y) axis text box. Key **Net Sales**.

9. At the top, select the Legend tab. Click in the Show legend check box to de-select the legend. Click Finish.

A line chart is printed that shows the Net Sales trend over the 10 year period.

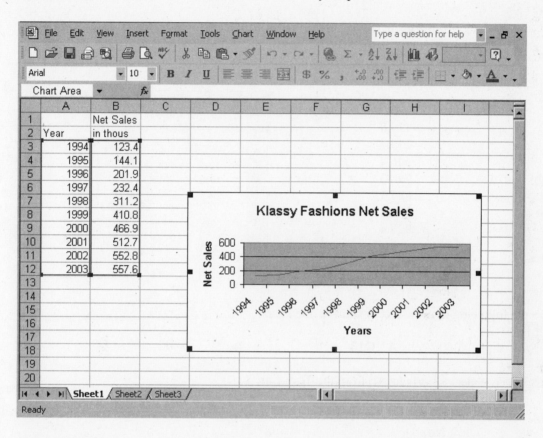

10. To make the chart larger and easier to read, click on the middle handle of the top line and drag the line to row 1.

You will now erase just the chart so that you can add more information to the problem.

11. To erase just the chart make sure the handles show on the chart box.

12. Push the <Delete> key.

The chart should now be erased.

Adding additional information:

Example 6. Assume the previous net sales figures are for Klassy Fashions Store in Memphis. Assume they opened a new store in Dallas in 1996. Add the new information so you can compare the net sales for the two stores.

1. Click your mouse arrow anywhere in row 3. Select Insert from the Menu bar. Select Rows. A new row is inserted above the sales figures.

2. Key **Memphis** in cell B3 and key **Dallas** in cell C3.

3. Starting with cell C6, key in the following values.

		A	B	C	D
123.2	1		Net Sales		
179.8	2	Year	in thous		
279.4	3		Memphis	Dallas	
506.4	4	1994	123.4		
798.3	5	1995	144.1		
887.1	6	1996	201.9	123.2	
916.2	7	1997	232.4	179.8	
928.4	8	1998	311.2	279.4	
	9	1999	410.8	506.4	
	10	2000	466.9	798.3	
	11	2001	512.7	887.1	
	12	2002	552.8	916.2	
	13	2003	557.6	928.4	

Do the following to make a comparative line chart:

4. Highlight cells **A3:C13**.

5. Select ChartWizard from the Tool bar.

6. In Step 1, under Chart type, select Line. Under Chart sub-type, select the upper left chart. Click Next.

7. In Step 2, at the top, select the Series tab. Under the Series list box, **Memphis** and **Dallas** should be listed. At the bottom, in the Category (X) axis labels text box, **=Sheet1!$A$4:$A$13** should already be entered. This identifies the first column as the x-axis labels. Click Next.

8. In Step 3, at the top, the Titles tab should be selected. Click on the Chart title text box, key **Comparison Chart Memphis and Dallas.** Tab to the Category (X) axis text box. Key **Years**. Tab to the Value (Y) axis text box. Key **Net Sales**. Click Finish.

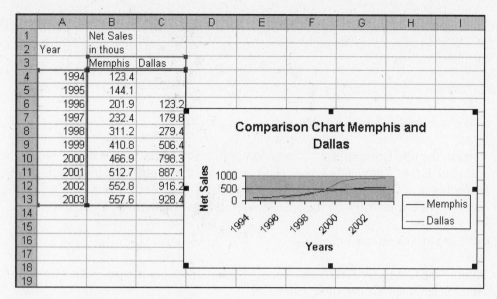

To enlarge the chart, drag the middle handle of the top line to row 1. To move the chart so you can see all the data, move your mouse arrow inside the chart. Click hold and drag the chart so the right side of the chart just touches the right side of column I.

Example 7. To show additional comparisons do the following:

1. Make sure the handles show on the chart box.

2. Click your **right** mouse arrow on one of the net sales lines. There will be a series of boxes along the line.

3. Select Format Data Series. At the top select the Options tab. Select the check box for Up-down bars. Click OK.

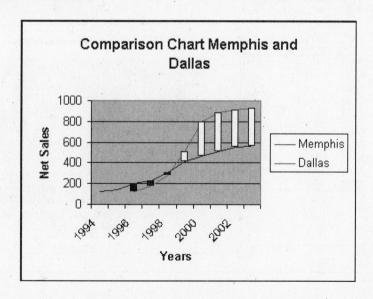

With the comparison line chart you can easily see that the Dallas store sold less than the Memphis store in 1996 when it first opened, but it soon started selling a much greater amount than Memphis.

Refining your chart

You can make changes to your chart to give it a different look.

1. Make sure the handles show on the chart.

2. Point to the title Comparison Chart Memphis and Dallas. A small box below the arrow will read, Chart Title. Click your **right** mouse on the Chart Title of Comparison Chart Memphis and Dallas. Select Format Chart Title. Select the Font tab. Under the Size column click your arrow on the up arrow scroll bar. Highlight **8**. Click OK.

The title is small and all fits on one line.

3. Point to the Category Axis Title, Years. **Right** Click your mouse. Select Format Axis Title. Select the font size of **8**. Click OK.

4. Do the same procedure for the Value Axis Title of Net Sales, the Value Axis of the sales and the Category Axis of the years. Select the font size of **8** for all titles.

5. Click on the Legend. It will have handles around it. Click, hold and drag the box down to the bottom right corner of the chart.

6. Click your arrow in the middle of the Plot Area. Place your arrow on the middle handle of the right side of the Plot Area and pull it to the right. Place your arrow on the middle handle of the top line of the Plot Area and pull it up to just below the Chart Title.

These steps allow you to make the graph area larger and easier to read.

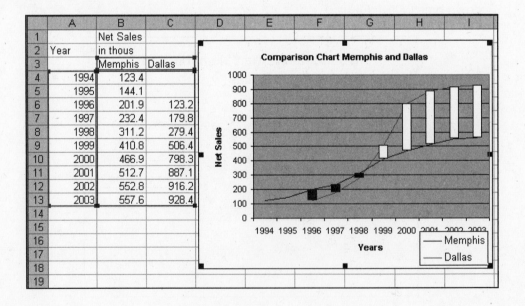

Suppose you want a different Chart Title.

7. Make sure the handles show on the chart.

8. Click on the Chart Title. There will be a box around the title. Key **Memphis and Dallas Sales**. As you key, the new title shows in the equation box. Push the <Enter> key. The new title is displayed on the chart.

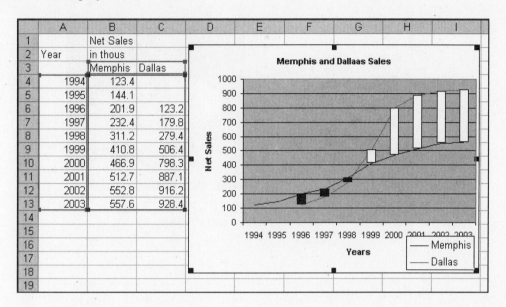

You can do the same with the X and Y- axis titles.

Experiment with your graphs to make them appear as you wish.

If you wish, save as **chart-3**. Close your file.

As shown below, Microsoft *Excel's ChartWizard* includes several other chart types. Within each of these types or categories of charts, you can choose a variation of the basic charts. They also allow you to view your data differently and experiment with your graphic presentations.

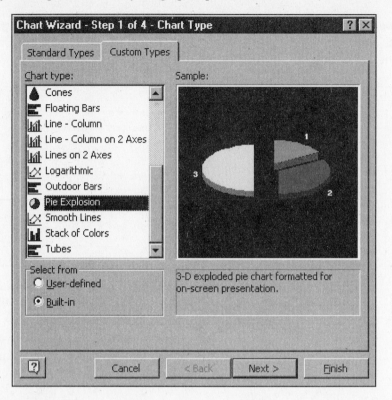

Embedding Charts in a Report

When creating a report describing data, it is often helpful to include a visual illustration. Excel allows you to embed sheets, or charts of information into a Microsoft Word document.

1. Open Microsoft Word for Windows.

2. Prepare your report leaving room for your Excel object. For this report key **The Clayton County Commissioners want to design a chart to show the taxpayers attending the forthcoming meeting what happens to their tax dollars.**

3. From the Menu bar, select File. Select Save As. In the Save in dialog box, make sure 3 ½ Floppy (A:) is selected. In the File name text box, key **budget**. Click Save.

4. Minimize Word by clicking on the minimize box in the top right corner of your screen. It looks like a box with a small line at the bottom.

5. Open Microsoft Excel if you are not already in it. Create the report you want to use in your Word document. In this case you will retrieve a file you created earlier.

6. From the Menu bar, select File. Select Open. Select pie-chart. Click Open.

7. Highlight **A1:I16**, to highlight the data and/or chart. From the Menu bar, select Edit. Select Cut. Minimize Excel by clicking on the minimize box in the top right hand corner of your screen.

8. Activate Word again by clicking on the Microsoft Word bar at the bottom of the screen.

9. Position your cursor at the point you wish to insert the report. From the Menu bar select Edit. Select Paste Special. Select Microsoft Excel Worksheet Object. Click on OK.

10. Place your mouse arrow on the chart. You can move the chart by clicking and dragging, or you can resize the chart with the handles.

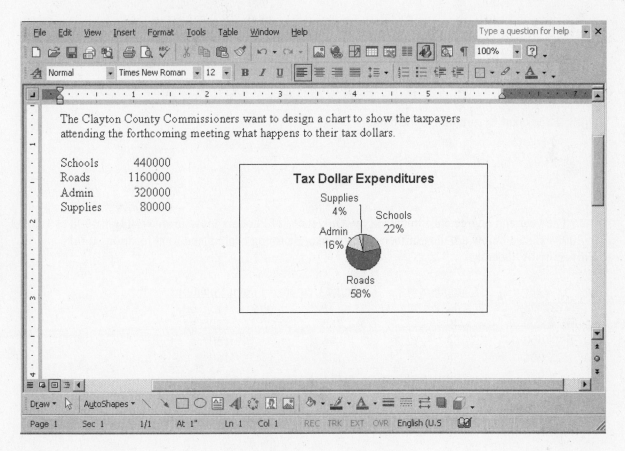

Save your file as **budget**. Close your file. Minimize Word. Open Excel.

Practice Exercises taken from textbook. (Put all related data in a single column.)

2-1. A headline in the Toledo Blade, reported that crime was on the decline. Listed below are the number of homicides from 1986 to 2002. (Textbook problem 2-19)

Year	Homicides	Year	Homicides
1986	21	1995	35
1987	34	1996	30
1988	26	1997	28
1989	42	1998	25
1990	37	1999	21
1991	37	2000	19
1992	44	2001	23
1993	45	2002	27
1994	40		

Draw a line chart to summarize the data.

2-2. The year end degree enrollments at the University of Phoenix grew from 71,400 in 1998 to 157,800 in 2002. Listed below are the numbers of campuses, learning centers and total locations for the University of Phoenix.

Year	Campuses	Learning Centers	Total Locations
1998	42	71	113
1999	49	80	129
2000	54	96	150
2001	58	102	160
2002	65	111	176

Source: Apollo Group, Inc. 2002 Annual Report

Use an appropriate chart to portray the data.

2-3. The following frequency distribution represents the number of days during a year that employees at the E. J. Wilcox Manufacturing Company were absent from work due to illness.

Number of days absent	Number of employees
0 up to 3	5
3 up to 6	12
6 up to 9	23
9 up to 12	8
12 up to 15	2
Total	50

Construct a histogram.

2-4. A recent survey showed that the typical American car owner spends $2,950 per year on operating expenses. Below is a breakdown of the various expenditure items. Draw an appropriate chart to portray the data. (Textbook problem 2-31) Hint: Abbreviate the Expenditure items to fit in one column.

Expenditure item	Amount
Fuel	$603
Interest on car loan	279
Repairs	930
Insurance and license	646
Depreciation	492
Total	$2,950

CHAPTER

3

DESCRIBING DATA: NUMERICAL MEASURES

CHAPTER GOALS

After completing this chapter, you will be able to:

1. Explain the characteristics and uses of measures of location.

2. Use Excel to calculate the arithmetic mean, median, mode, geometric mean and the weighted mean.

3. Explain the characteristics and uses of measurements of dispersion.

4. Use Excel's Descriptive Statistics Analysis ToolPak to find measures of location and dispersion.

5. Define each measurement found in Excel's Descriptive Statistics Analysis ToolPak Output Table.

Introduction

Over 100 years ago H. G. Wells noted that "statistical thinking will one day be as necessary for efficient citizenship as the ability to read and write." That day has arrived. Today, we cannot avoid being bombarded with all sorts of numerical data. Statistical techniques are used extensively in almost all career fields: social science, physical science, marketing, accounting, quality control, health science, education, professional sports, and politics to name just a few. This chapter will show how easy it is to use Excel to find measures of location (central tendency) and dispersion, measures that are essential to using and understanding statistical data.

Measures of Location: We will use Excel to find a single value or an average to describe a set of data. This single value is referred to as a measure of location. We often need a single number to represent a set of data – one number that can be thought of as being "typical" of all the data. Most people think of arithmetic mean when they hear the word average. However, there are several measures that show the central value of a set of data. The measures of location shown in this chapter that you can use Excel commands to find are the arithmetic mean, the median, the mode, and the geometric mean. We will also create a template to find weighted mean.

The **arithmetic mean** is the most commonly used measure of central tendency. When you total your examination grades and divide by the number of exams, you have computed the arithmetic mean, or average. What follows is an example of how to compute a mean using this formula. For example, during an agonizing quarter, Sam Wise received the following grades on 9 exams in college algebra (arranged in scending order): 2, 7, 11, 20, 30, 40, 55, 71, and 71. Sam's mean semester grade, then, was $(2+7+11+20+30+40+55+71+71) \div 9 = 34.111$ or 34, rounded.

The **median** is a measurement of position. If you arrange a series of values in either ascending or descending order, the middle figure in the array of values is called the median. In the case of Sam's grades, the middle or median grade was 30. Both the mean grade of 34 and the median grade of 30 seem to reveal the same thing: Sam was having great difficulty grasping algebra. Even if Sam's instructor had thrown out Sam's lowest grade, the median grade would have been halfway between 30 and 40, that is, 35, not much change. While Sam's mean grade of 34 differed only slightly from his median grade of 30, it is possible in other cases for the difference between the mean and the median to be substantial.

The **mode** is defined as the most frequently occurring value in a series. In the example of Sam's grade, the mode is 71 (a value that might appeal to Sam, but not his teacher). Although not especially useful in our example, the mode is important to, say, the department store buyer of men's suits who wants to order the most popular styles, colors, and sizes.

The **geometric mean** is useful in finding the average of relative numbers such as percentages, ratios, indexes, or growth rates. Suppose a company, say Zane Marketing, had sales increases of 3.2 percent, 1.5 percent, 4.8 percent and 38.5 percent. The average percent increase as shown below would be 11.0 which is different than the arithmetic mean of 12.0.

$$GM = \sqrt[n]{(x_1)(x_2)...(x_n)}$$

$$GM = \sqrt[4]{(1.032)(1.015)(1.048)(1.385)}$$

$$GM = 1.11042 \ or \ 11.0\%$$

The geometric mean will always be less than or equal to (never more than) the arithmetic mean. Note also that all data values must be positive to determine the geometric mean.

The **weighted mean** is a special case of the arithmetic mean. It occurs when one value has more importance or more weight than another. For example, a five credit statistics class is more important to your grade point average (GPA) than a one credit bowling course. If Jose earned a 3.2 in his five credits of statistics, 2.8 in four credits of speech, 3.7 in three credits of literature, and 4.0 in a one credit bowling course, what is his GPA?

$$\bar{x}_w = \frac{\Sigma(wx)}{\Sigma x}$$

$$\bar{x}_w = \frac{(5\times3.2)+(4\times2.8)+(3\times3.7)+(1\times4.0)}{5+4+3+1}$$

$$\bar{x}_w = 3.25385 \ or \ 3.3$$

Measures of Dispersion. If two distributions have the same mean, median, and mode, is there no difference between the distributions? Not necessarily. The distributions below are normal, unimodal, symmetrical, bell (or mound) shaped. They have the same measures of central tendency, but they are not identical. Distribution A has more spread, a greater dispersion or variability than distribution B.

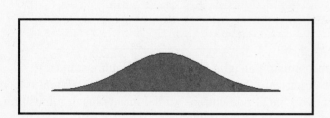

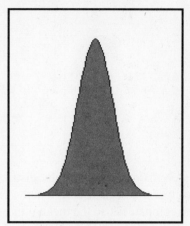

Distribution A   Distribution B

The following is an illustration to help understand the importance of dispersion. An English teacher being pressured to coach a track team does some checking and finds that: the four high-jumpers can only clear an average of 4 feet, the three pole vaulters can only manage an average height of 9 feet, and the average runner can only run the mile in 8 minutes. He concludes that he does not want to manage such a certain failure. Is his assessment accurate? Maybe, but not from the data he collected. Had he looked further, he would have found that one of the four high-jumpers consistently clears 7 feet (good enough for any competition he might face) while the others stumble over 3-foot heights. In the pole vault, one athlete vaults 15 feet, while the others barely explode over a 6-foot bar. And the team has one runner who can break a 4-minute mile. The moral of this tale: without knowledge of dispersion, averages alone do not give a complete picture.

Remember, if one of your feet is frozen in ice (0 degrees Celsius) and the other in almost boiling water (74 degrees Celsius), on average you should be a comfortable 37 degrees Celsius body temperature.

The simplest measure of dispersion is **range**, which is the difference between the highest and lowest values. The most common statistical measurement of dispersion is the **standard deviation** (σ) for population data, and s for sample data, or expressed another way, s is used to approximate σ . The standard deviation is the positive square root of the variance. The variance is the measure of the average squared deviations between each observation and the mean. But what is standard deviation? What does it do, and what does it mean? The above definition really doesn't tell much. Perhaps a better way of defining standard deviation is by looking at how it is applied to the many areas where it is useful.

The empirical rule as illustrated below is a guideline which states, when a distribution of data is normally distributed or approximately mound-shaped, about 68 percent of the data values fall within one standard deviation of the mean, 95 percent fall within two standard deviations, and almost 100 percent (99.7) within three standard deviations

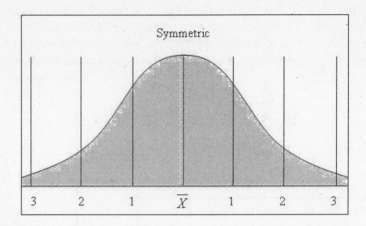

Because many phenomena are distributed approximately in a bell shape, including most human characteristics such as height and weight, the empirical rule is widely used. In the area of quality control, many companies use the mean plus or minus two standard deviations, or the mean plus or minus three standard deviations as cutoff points for acceptance or rejection guidelines.

For example, in 2000 the average fuel consumption rate of automobiles in the United States was 21.2 miles per gallon. If the standard deviation was 5.9 mpg we could use the empirical rule to estimate the distribution of fuel rates of automobiles. About two-thirds (68%) of the fuel consumption rates would fall between 15.3 mpg and 27.1 mpg (21.2 ± 5.9). Ninety-five percent of the fuel rates would fall between 9.4 and 33.0 (21.2 ± two times 5.9). And almost all of the automobiles would have fuel rates between 3.5 and 38.9 mpg (21.2 ± three times 5.9).

Understanding standard deviation is important in statistics.

- It is the most frequently used measure of dispersion. Because of the mathematical properties it possesses, it's more suitable than any other measure of dispersion involving statistical inference procedures.

- It is affected by the value of every observation in a series. A change in the value of any observation will change the standard deviation value. Its value may be distorted by a relatively few extreme values.

- It is often used for making control charts, since most control charts are based on the fact that 95 percent of the normal distribution will fall within plus or minus two standard deviations of the mean. Any item in the distribution that is less than two standard deviations from the mean is considered in control. The difference is attributed to sampling error and chance within the process being used. Any item outside the plus or minus two standard deviations is considered out of control. The difference is attributed to some assignable cause that could be corrected.

Example 1. (mean, median and mode)

Cambridge Power and Light Company selected 20 residential customers. Following are the amounts, to the nearest dollar, the customers were charged for electrical services last month:

54	48	58	50	25	47	75	46	60	70
67	68	39	35	56	66	33	62	65	67

What are the mean, median and mode of these amounts?

1. On a new worksheet, key your data in column A. Key **Example 1** in A1, **Amounts** in A3 and the numbers in A4:A23.

2. In A24:A26, key the labels: **Mean=**, **Median=**, and **Mode=** respectively. Your sheet will look like the example on the right.

In the cell to the right of each label, key the formulas.

3. In B24, key =**AVERAGE(A4:A23)**. Excel uses *average* for the *arithmetic mean*.

4. In B25, key =**MEDIAN(A4:A23)**

5. In B26, key =**MODE(A4:A23)**

Bold the contents of A1. Bold the contents of B24:B26.

	A	B
1	**Example 1**	
2		
3	Amounts	
4	54	
5	48	
6	58	
7	50	
8	25	
9	47	
10	75	
11	46	
12	60	
13	70	
14	67	
15	68	
16	39	
17	35	
18	56	
19	66	
20	33	
21	62	
22	65	
23	67	
24	Mean=	
25	Median=	
26	Mode=	
27		

	A	B	C
1	**Example 1**		
2			
3	Amounts		
4	54		
5	48		
6	58		
7	50		
8	25		
9	47		
10	75		
11	46		
12	60		
13	70		
14	67		
15	68		
16	39		
17	35		
18	56		
19	66		
20	33		
21	62		
22	65		
23	67		
24	Mean=	54.55	
25	Median=	57	
26	Mode=	67	
27			

The output is as follows:

The average or mean is *54.55*. The median is *57*. (Since there is an even number of data there is no single middle number. The median is the average of the middle *two* numbers, 54 and 60). The mode is *67*.

If there is *no* mode, Excel will display #N/A in that cell. If there is *more than one* mode Excel will display the one that occurs first in the string of data.

Put your data in a single column. Be sure to include within the parentheses the cell references that contain the data.

Chapter 3

Example 2. (geometric mean)

The profits earned by Atkins Construction Company on four recent projects were 3 percent, 2 percent, 4 percent, and 6 percent. What is the geometric mean profit?

1. On your same worksheet, key **Example 2** in C1 and **Percent Profit** in C3.

2. In C4:C7, key **3,2,4**, and **6** respectively.

3. In C8:C10, key **Geometric**, **mean**, and **profit=** respectively.

4. In D10, key =**GEOMEAN(C4:C7)**.

Bold the contents of C1 and D10.

Your sheet should look as follows:

	A	B	C	D	E	F	G	H	I
1	Example 1		Example 2						
2									
3	Amounts		Precent Profit						
4	54		3						
5	48		2						
6	58		4						
7	50		6						
8	25		Geometric						
9	47		mean						
10	75		profit=	3.464102					
11	46								
12	60								
13	70								
14	67								
15	68								
16	39								
17	35								
18	56								
19	66								
20	33								
21	62								
22	65								
23	67								
24	Mean=	54.55							
25	Median=	57							
26	Mode=	67							

Sheet1 / Sheet2 / Sheet3

Ready

NUM

38

Example 3. (using geometric mean to find an average percent increase over a period of time)

During the decade of the 1990's, Las Vegas, Nevada, was the fastest growing metropolitan area in the United States. The population increased from 852,737 in 1990 to 1,563,282 in 2000. This is an increase of 710,545 people or an 83 percent increase over the 10-year period. What is the average annual increase?

The formula for finding the average percent increase over a period of time is:

$$\sqrt[n]{\frac{\text{Value at end of Period}}{\text{Value at start of Period}}} - 1$$

1. On your same worksheet, key **Example 3** in C12.

2. In C14:C17, key **ending value =, beginning value =, period of time =** and **geometric mean** = respectively.

3. In E14:E16 key **1563282, 852737** and **10** respectively

4. In E17, key **=((E14/E15)^(1/E16))-1**

5. Highlight **E17**. From the tool bar choose Format. Choose Cells. Under Category, choose Percentage. Click OK.

The population of Las Vegas increased at a rate of 6.25 percent per year from 1990 to 2000.

The ^ symbol is the number 6 with the shift key. It symbolizes "the power of". When the ^ symbol is used with a fraction, 1/n, it takes the nth root of the number proceeding it.

Bold the contents of C12 and E17.

Your worksheet will look as follows.

	A	B	C	D	E	F
1	Example 1		Example 2			
2						
3	Amounts		Percent Profit			
4	54		3			
5	48		2			
6	58		4			
7	50		6			
8	25		Geometric			
9	47		mean			
10	75		profit=	3.464102		
11	46					
12	60		Example 3			
13	70					
14	67		ending value=		1563282	
15	68		beginning value =		852737	
16	39		period of time =		10	
17	35		geometric mean=		6.25%	
18	56					
19	66					
20	33					
21	62					
22	65					
23	67					
24	Mean=	54.55				
25	Median=	57				
26	Mode=	67				
27						

Formula view allows you to view the formulas and functions within a cell, rather than the output value. To toggle between normal view and formula view, hold down the control key while tapping the tilde key (located above the tab key on most keyboards). You may have to adjust the column width to be able to view the entire formula.

The following is an example of the same page in formula view.

Remember: to switch back to normal view, hold down the control key and tap the tilde key.

	A	B	C	D	E	F	G	H
1	Example 1		Example 2					
2								
3	Amounts		Percent Profit					
4	54		3					
5	48		2					
6	58		4					
7	50		6					
8	25		Geometric					
9	47		mean					
10	75		profit=	=GEOMEAN(C4:C7)				
11	46							
12	60		Example 3					
13	70							
14	67		ending value=		1563282			
15	68		beginning value =		852737			
16	39		period of time =		10			
17	35		geometric mean=		=((E14/E15)^(1/E16))			
18	56							
19	66							
20	33							
21	62							
22	65							
23	67							
24	Mean=	=AVERAGE(A4:A23)						
25	Median=	=MEDIAN(A4:A23)						
26	Mode=	=MODE(A4:A23)						
27								

Cell E17 formula bar: f_x =((E14/E15)^(1/E16))-1

Example 4. (weighted mean)

Carter Construction Company pays its hourly employees either $11.50, $13.50, or $15.50 per hour. There are 26 hourly employees, 14 are paid at the $11.50 rate, 10 at the $13.50 rate, and 2 at the $15.50 rate. What is the weighted mean hourly rate paid the 26 employees?

1. In F1, key **Example 4**

2. Key **Employee** in F3, **Rate** in G3, **Product** in H3, **Weighted** in F8 and **mean**= in F9.

Your worksheet will look as follows:

	A	B	C	D	E	F	G	H
1	**Example 1**		**Example 2**			Example 4		
2								
3	Amounts		Percent Profit			Employee	Rate	Product
4	54		3					
5	48		2					
6	58		4					
7	50		6					
8	25		Geometric			Weighted		
9	47		mean			mean=		
10	75		profit=	**3.464102**				
11	46							
12	60		**Example 3**					
13	70							
14	67		ending value=		1563282			
15	68		beginning value =		852737			
16	39		period of time =		10			
17	35		geometric mean=		**6.25%**			
18	56							
19	66							
20	33							
21	62							
22	65							
23	67							
24	Mean=	**54.55**						
25	Median=	**57**						
26	Mode=	**67**						
27								

3. Key **14,10**, and **2** in F4:F6 respectively

4. Key **11.5**, **13.5**, and **15.5** in G4:G6 respectively.

5. In H4, key =**F4*G4**.

6. Make H4 your active cell. Place your cursor on the bottom right handle. You will have a thick black plus sign. Click and drag to H5:H6.

7. Highlight **F4:F6**. From the Tool bar choose the AutoSum button.

8. Highlight **H4:H6**. From the Tool bar choose the AutoSum button.

9. In G9, key =**H7/F7**.

Bold the contents of F1 and G9. Your output will look as follows.

	A	B	C	D	E	F	G	H
1	**Example 1**		Example 2			**Example 4**		
2								
3	Amounts		Percent Profit			Employee	Rate	Product
4	54		3			14	11.5	161
5	48		2			10	13.5	135
6	58		4			2	15.5	31
7	50		6			26		327
8	25		Geometric			Weighted		
9	47		mean			mean=	**12.57692**	
10	75		profit=	3.464102				
11	46							
12	60		**Example 3**					
13	70							
14	67		ending value=	1563282				
15	68		beginning value =	852737				
16	39		period of time =	10				
17	35		geometric mean=	**6.25%**				
18	56							
19	66							
20	33							
21	62							
22	65							
23	67							
24	Mean=	**54.55**						
25	Median=	**57**						
26	Mode=	**67**						
27								

Excel's Descriptive Statistics Analysis ToolPak allows you to find the mean, standard error, median, mode, standard deviation, sample variance, kurtosis, skewness, range, minimum, maximum, sum, count, largest number by position, smallest number by position, and the level of confidence simply by entering the numerical data. If Analysis Tools doesn't appear in the Add-Ins available list box, you may need to add the Analysis ToolPak using a custom installation of the Microsoft Excel Setup program.

To demonstrate how to use Excel to compute measures of central tendency and dispersion, here is a typical example:

Dave's Automatic Door Installations installs automatic garage door openers. The following list indicates the number of minutes needed to install a sample of 10 doors: 28, 32, 24, 46, 44, 40, 54, 38, 32, and 42.

1. On a new worksheet, key your data in column A. From the Menu bar, select Tools. If Data Analysis does not appear, select Add-Ins. Select Analysis ToolPak. Click OK.

2. From the Menu bar, select Tools. Select Data Analysis. Select Descriptive Statistics. Click on OK.

3. For Input Range:, key **A1:A11**. Or you may click your mouse on cell A1 then hold and drag to highlight cells A1:A11. Your input range will vary depending on the number in your sample.

4. Grouped by Columns should be selected.

5. Select Labels in First Row. If the first row does not contain a label, make sure that the check box is not selected.

6. Select Confidence Level for Mean. Select the text box. In this instance, key in **90**.

7. Select Kth Largest. Select the text box. In this instance, key in **2**.

8. Select Kth Smallest. Select the text box. In this instance, key in **2**.

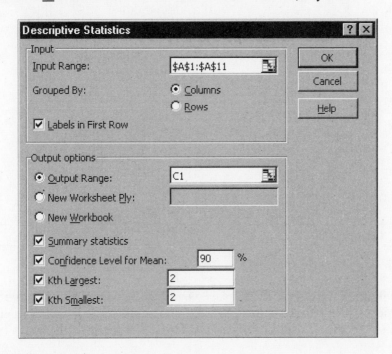

9. Select Output Range. Select the text box, key in **C1**.

(New Worksheet Ply and New Workbook should not be selected.)

10. Select Summary statistics. Click on OK.

The descriptive statistics have been computed automatically.

HINT: After you get your results, cross-check the *count* in the output table to make sure it contains the correct number of sample items.

	A	B	C	D
1	Minutes		*Minutes*	
2	28			
3	32		Mean	38
4	24		Standard E	2.875181
5	46		Median	39
6	44		Mode	32
7	40		Standard D	9.092121
8	54		Sample Va	82.66667
9	38		Kurtosis	-0.43626
10	32		Skewness	0.133047
11	42		Range	30
12			Minimum	24
13			Maximum	54
14			Sum	380
15			Count	10
16			Largest(2)	46
17			Smallest(2	28
18			Confidence	5.270534
19				

To make your chart easier to read do the following:

1. Place your mouse arrow in the column heading between columns C, and D. The arrow will change to a thick black plus sign. Double click your left mouse button. Column C will automatically widen to accommodate the longest description.

2. Activate cell D4. From the Tool bar, place your mouse pointer on **Decrease Decimal** icon. Click your left mouse button three times. The Standard Deviation is now rounded to three decimals places and is easier to read.

3. Format cells, D7, D8, D9, D10, and D18 to all have three decimal places.

The chart is now easier to read.

	A	B	C	D	E
1	Minutes		Minutes		
2	28				
3	32		Mean	38	
4	24		Standard Error	2.875	
5	46		Median	39	
6	44		Mode	32	
7	40		Standard Deviation	9.092	
8	54		Sample Variance	82.667	
9	38		Kurtosis	-0.436	
10	32		Skewness	0.133	
11	42		Range	30	
12			Minimum	24	
13			Maximum	54	
14			Sum	380	
15			Count	10	
16			Largest(2)	46	
17			Smallest(2)	28	
18			Confidence Level(90.0%)	5.271	
19					

Chapter 3 focuses on measures of location (or central tendency) and dispersion but since the output table displays additional terms that we use in future chapters, we have taken this opportunity to define what Excel displays.

Excel's Descriptive Statistics Output Table contains three measures of location: mean, median and mode. The **Mean** (38) is computed by dividing the sum (380) by the count (10).

The **Median** (39) is a measurement of position in a ranked set of data. It is the middle number in a data set with an odd number of values. In an even set of numbers, it is the value halfway between the two middle values.

The **Mode** (32) is a measurement of frequency, it is the most frequently occurring value. When there are two or more values that appear the same number of times (duplicate modes), Excel reports the value that appears first in the data set. In some data sets, each value is unique so Excel reports "#N/A." The mode is often used with grouped data. A frequency distribution with the highest number of occurrences is called the modal interval.

The output table contains several measures of variation. The **Range** (30) equals the **Maximum** value(54) minus the **Minimum** value(24). Remember, with some data sets the range can be a misleading measure of variation since it only contains the two most extreme values.

The **Standard Deviation** (9.092) is the most common measure of variation or dispersion. In a normal or symmetrical set of data about 68 percent will be within plus or minus one standard deviation of the mean (28.908 - 47.092), 95 percent will be within plus or minus two standard deviations of the mean (19.816 - 56.184), and almost all of the data (99.7 percent) will be within plus or minus three standard deviations of the mean (10.724 - 65.276).

The **Variance** is the standard deviation squared. Excel's output table shows the sample standard deviation and variance computed using *n-1* in the denominator. To find the *population* standard deviation and the *population* variance, computed by using *n* as the denominator, use the STDEVP and VARP functions.

The **Largest (2)** and the **Smallest (2)** values in Excel's output table are the second longest (46) and the second shortest (28) installation times. These values can be used to eliminate outliers. They can also be use to estimate quartiles in data with a large number of frequencies. For example if you had 1600 in your data set you would divide the count (1600) by 4 and enter 400 as the largest and the smallest. The output table would then show the approximate third and first quartile .

The **Standard Error** (2.875) shown on the output table will be used more extensively later in our exercises. The standard error is the standard deviation divided by the square root of the sample size. It is a measure of uncertainty about the mean, and is used for statistical inference (confidence intervals, regression belts, and hypothesis tests.)

The **Confidence Level (90.0%)** (5.271) is half of the 90% confidence interval for the mean. In this measurement we can be 90% confident that the interval, 32.729 minutes to 43.271 minutes, will contain the population parameter or the true mean installation time.

Kurtosis (-0.436) measures the degree of peakedness in symmetric distributions. If a symmetric distribution is more peaked than the normal distribution, that is, if there are fewer values in the tails, the kurtosis measure is negative. If the distribution is flatter than the normal distribution, that is if there are more values in the tails than a corresponding normal distribution, the kurtosis measure is positive. (For more details on how Excel computes kurtosis search Help for "KURT function").

Skewness (0.133) is a measurement of the lack of symmetry in a distribution. If there are a few extreme small values and the tail of the distribution runs off to the left we say the distribution is negatively skewed and our skewness value would be negative. If there are a few extremely large values and the tail of the distribution runs off to the right, we say the distribution is positively skewed and the skewness value would be positive. The formula for finding skewness used by Excel is different than the Pearson's Coefficient of Skewness used in the Statistical Techniques in Business and Economics textbook. (Excel computes the skewness value using the third power of the deviations from the mean. For more details on how Excel computes skewness search Help for "SKEW function").

Practice Exercises taken from textbook. (Put all related data in a single column.)

3-1. The accounting firm of Crawford and Associates has five senior partners. Yesterday the senior partners saw six, four, three, seven, and five clients respectively. Compute the mean number and median number of clients seen by a partner. (Textbook Problem 3-59)

3-2. Owens Orchards sells apples in a large bag by weight. A sample of seven bags contained the following number of apples: 23, 19, 26, 17, 21, 24, 22. Compute the mean number and median number of apples in a bag. (Textbook Problem 3-60)

3-3. Trudy Green works for the True-Green Lawn Company. Her job is to solicit lawn-care business via the telephone. Listed below is the number of appointments she made in each of the last 25 hours of calling. (Textbook Problem 3-64)

9	5	2	6	5	6	4	4	7	2	3	6	3
4	4	7	8	4	4	5	5	4	8	3	3	

What is the arithmetic mean number of appointments she made per hour? What is the median number of appointments per hour?

3-4. The American Automobile Association checks the prices of gasoline before many holiday weekends. Listed below is the self-serve price for a sample of 15 retail outlets during the May 2003 Memorial Day weekend, in the Detroit, Michigan area. (Textbook Problem 3-68)

1.44	1.42	1.35	1.39	1.49	1.49	1.41	1.46
1.41	1.49	1.45	1.48	1.39	1.46	1.44	

    a.   What is the arithmetic mean selling price?
    b.   What is the median selling price?
    c.   What is the modal selling price?

3-5. Compute the geometric mean of the following percent increases: 8, 12, 14, 26, and 5. (Textbook Problem 3-23)

3-6. Listed below is the percent increase in sales for the MG Corporation over the last 5 years. Determine the geometric mean percent increase in sales over the period. (Textbook Problem 3-25)

9.4%, 13.8%, 11.7%, 11.9%, 14.7%

3-7. The Loris Healthcare System employs 200 persons on the nursing staff. Fifty are nurse's aids, 50 are practical nurses, and 100 are registered nurses. Nurse's aids receive $8 an hour, practical nurses $15 an hour, and registered nurses $24 an hour. What is the weighted mean hourly wage? (Textbook Problem 3-13)

3-8. The Split-A-Rail Fence Company sells three types of fences to homeowners in suburban Seattle, Washington. Grade A costs $5.00 per running foot to install, Grade B costs $6.50 per running foot, and Grade C, the premium quality, costs $8.00 per running foot. Yesterday, Split-A-Rail installed 270 feet of Grade A, 300 feet of Grade B, and 100 feet of Grade C. What was the weighted mean cost per foot of fence installed? (Textbook Problem 3-65)

3-9. The metropolitan area of Los Angeles-Long Beach, California, is the area expected to show the largest increase in the number of jobs between 1989 and 2010. The number of jobs is expected to increase from 5,164,900 to 6,286,800. What is the geometric mean expected yearly rate of increase? (Textbook Problem 3-69)

3-10. A sample of households that subscribe to the United Bell Phone Company revealed the following numbers of calls received last week: (Textbook Problem 3-61)

| 52 | 43 | 30 | 38 | 30 | 42 | 12 | 46 |
| 39 | 37 | 34 | 46 | 32 | 18 | 41 | 5 |

Using a confidence level of 95%, and a largest and smallest K of 4, use Excel to find the measures of central tendency and dispersion.

3-11. Listed below are the number of lampshades produced during the last 50 days at the American Lampshade Company in Rockville, GA: (Textbook Problem 3-63)

348	371	360	369	376	397	368	361	374	410
374	377	335	356	322	344	399	362	384	365
380	349	358	343	432	376	347	385	399	400
359	329	370	398	352	396	366	392	375	379
389	390	386	341	351	354	395	338	390	333

Using a confidence level of 90%, and a largest and smallest K of 10, use Excel to find the measures of central tendency and dispersion.

CHAPTER
4
DESCRIBING DATA: DISPLAYING AND EXPLORING DATA

CHAPTER GOALS

After completing this chapter, you will be able to:

1. Develop and interpret quartiles, deciles and percentiles.

2. Compute and understand the coefficient of skewness.

3. Define the measurements found in Excel's Descriptive Statistics Analysis ToolPak Output Table.

4. Use Excel to draw and interpret a scatter diagram.

Introduction

Chapter 3 introduced you to several measures of location such as the mean and the median that allow us to report a typical value in a set of observations. You also computed several measures of dispersion such as mean and standard deviation that allow us to describe the variation or spread in a set of data. We continue with descriptive statistics in this chapter.

Although the standard deviation is the most used measure of dispersion it is sometimes useful to divide a set of observations into equal parts and measure positions using **quartiles**, **deciles** or **percentiles**. The first, second and third quartiles divide a set of observations into four equal parts. Remember in Chapter 3 when we arranged a set of data from smallest to largest the middle point was the median. When we arrange a set of data from smallest to largest and divide it into 4 equal parts the value below which 25 percent of the observations occur is the first quartile. The middle point, the median, is the second quartile. The value below which 75 percent of the observations occur is the third quartile. The middle 50 percent of the data, the **quartile range**, is between the first quartile and the third quartile.

Deciles and percentiles are also measurements of position. After arranging the data into an ordered array from smallest to largest if we divide it into 10 equal parts we have deciles and if we divide it into 100 equal parts we have percentiles. If your income was in the 7th decile you could conclude that 70 percent of the people have a lower income and 30 percent have a higher income. If your friend finished in the 42nd percentile in the Boston Marathon then she finished ahead of 42 percent of the runners and behind 58 percent of the runners

Another characteristic of a set of data is its shape. The shape is **symmetrical** if the mean and the median are the same and the data is spread evenly so that the data values below and above the mean and median are mirror images of each other such as the illustrations of dispersion in Chapter 3. The shape is positively skewed when the mean is larger than the median and the values extend further to the right of the peak. The shape is negatively skewed when the mean is smaller than the median and the data extends further to the left of the peak. When a set of data has two peaks it is bimodal, three peaks tri-modal and etc.

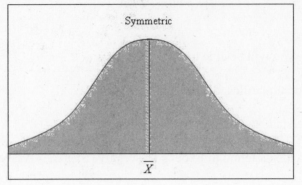

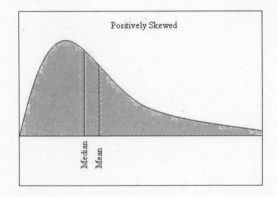

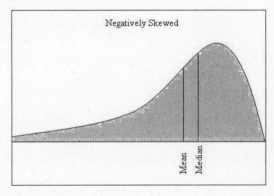

To demonstrate how to use Excel to compute measures of central tendency, dispersion, position and shape here is a typical example.

Example 1. The quality control department of the SummerSweet Jelly and Jam Company is responsible for checking the weight of the 8-ounce jars of Raspberry Jam. The weights of a sample of 13 jars are:

7.68   7.82   8.12   8.03   7.89   7.93   8.09   7.75   7.88   8.01   8.11   7.99   8.03

1. On a new worksheet, key your data in column A. From the Menu bar, select Tools. If Data Analysis does not appear, select Add-Ins. Select Analysis ToolPak. Click OK.

2. From the Menu bar, select Tools. Select Data Analysis. Select Descriptive Statistics. Click on OK.

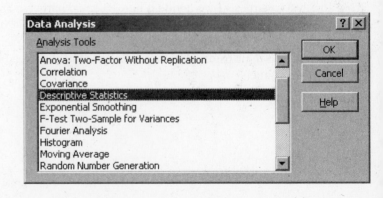

3. For Input Range:, key **A1:A14**. Or you may click your mouse on cell A1 then hold and drag to highlight cells A1:A14. Your input range will vary depending on the number in your sample.

4. Grouped by Columns, should be selected.

5. Select Labels in First Row. If the first row does not contain a label, make sure that the check box is not selected.

6. Select Output Range. Select the text box, key in **C1**.

7. Select Summary statistics. Click on OK.

8. Select Confidence Level for Mean. Select the text box, in this instance key in **90**.

```
Descriptive Statistics                                    ? X
 ┌─Input──────────────────────────────┐    ┌──────────┐
 │ Input Range:          $A$1:$A$14  ▨ │    │    OK    │
 │                                     │    └──────────┘
 │ Grouped By:        ● Columns        │    ┌──────────┐
 │                    ○ Rows           │    │  Cancel  │
 │                                     │    └──────────┘
 │ ☑ Labels in first row               │    ┌──────────┐
 │                                     │    │   Help   │
 └─────────────────────────────────────┘    └──────────┘
 ┌─Output options──────────────────────┐
 │ ● Output Range:        $C$1       ▨ │
 │ ○ New Worksheet Ply:                │
 │ ○ New Workbook                      │
 │ ☑ Summary statistics                │
 │ ☑ Confidence Level for Mean:  90  % │
 │ ☑ Kth Largest:          2           │
 │ ☑ Kth Smallest:         2           │
 └─────────────────────────────────────┘
```

9. Select Kth Largest. Select the text box, in this instance key in **2**.

10. Select Kth Smallest. Select the text box, in this instance key in **2**.

(New Worksheet Ply and New Workbook should not be selected.)

The descriptive statistics have been computed automatically.

HINT: After you get your results, cross-check the *count* in the output table to make sure it contains the correct number of sample items.

To make your chart easier to read do the following:

1. Place your mouse arrow in the column heading between columns C, and D. The arrow will change to a thick black plus sign. Double click your left mouse button. Column C will automatically widen to accommodate the longest description.

2. Place your mouse arrow in the column heading D. The arrow will be a thick down arrow. Click your left mouse button. The entire D column will be highlighted.

3. From the Menu bar, select Format. Select Cells. The Number tab should be selected.

4. Under Category:, select Number. In the Decimal places: text box, key in **3**. Or click on the up arrow to 3. Click on OK.

The chart is now easier to read.

	A	B	C	D	E
1	Weight		*Weight*		
2	7.68				
3	7.82		Mean	7.948	
4	8.12		Standard Error	0.038	
5	8.03		Median	7.990	
6	7.89		Mode	8.030	
7	7.93		Standard Deviation	0.139	
8	8.09		Sample Variance	0.019	
9	7.75		Kurtosis	-0.532	
10	7.88		Skewness	-0.603	
11	8.01		Range	0.440	
12	8.11		Minimum	7.680	
13	7.99		Maximum	8.120	
14	8.03		Sum	103.330	
15			Count	13.000	
16			Largest(2)	8.110	
17			Smallest(2)	7.750	
18			Confidence Level(90.0%)	0.069	
19					

Chapter 4 focuses on location and shape but since the output table displays additional terms, we have taken this opportunity to define what Excel displays, like we did in Chapter 3.

Excel's Descriptive Statistics Output Table contains three measures of central tendency: mean, median and mode. The **Mean** (7.948) is computed by dividing the sum (103.330) by the count (13).

The **Median** (7.990) is a measurement of position in a ranked set of data. It is the middle number in a data set with an odd number of values. In an even set of numbers, it is the value halfway between the two middle values.

The **Mode** (8.030) is a measurement of frequency, it is the most frequently occurring value. When there are two or more values that appear the same number of times (duplicate modes), Excel reports the value that appears first in the data set. In some data sets, each value is unique so Excel reports "#N/A." The mode is often used with grouped data. A frequency distribution with the highest number of occurrences is called the modal interval.

The output table contains several measures of variation. The **Range** (.440) equals the **Maximum** value (8.120) minus the **Minimum** value(7.680). Remember, with some data sets the range can be a misleading measure of variation since it only contains the two most extreme values.

The **Standard Deviation** (.139) is the most common measure of variation or dispersion. In a normal or symmetrical set of data about 68 percent will be within plus or minus one standard deviation of the mean (7.809 – 8.087), 95 percent will be within plus or minus two standard deviations of the mean (7.670 – 8.226), and almost all of the data (99.7 percent) will be within plus or minus three standard deviations of the mean (7.531 – 8.365).

The **Variance** is the standard deviation squared. Excel's output table shows the sample standard deviation and variance computed using *n-1* in the denominator. To find the *population* standard deviation and the *population* variance, computed by using *n* as the denominator, use the STDEVP and VARP functions.

The **Largest (2)** and the **Smallest (2)** values in Excel's output table are the second largest (8.110) and the second smallest (7.750) weight. These values can be used to eliminate outliers. They can also be use to estimate quartiles in data with a large number of frequencies. For example if you had 1600 in your data set you would divide the count (1600) by 4 and enter 400 as the largest and the smallest. The output table would then show the approximate third and first quartile. If the data is arranged in order from smallest to largest and you divide count (1600) by ten you would have the 160th item as the first decile and 1440th item as the ninth decile. You could also divide by 100 and estimate percentiles..

The **Standard Error** (0.038) shown on the output table will be used more extensively later in our exercises. The standard error is the standard deviation divided by the square root of the sample size. It is a measure of uncertainty about the mean, and is used for statistical inference (confidence intervals, regression belts, and hypothesis tests.)

The **Confidence Level (90.0%)** (.069) is half of the 90% confidence interval for the mean. In this measurement we can be 90% confident that the interval, 7.879 ounces to 8.017 ounces, will contain the population parameter or the true mean weight.

Kurtosis (-0.532) measures the degree of peakedness in symmetric distributions. If a symmetric distribution is more peaked than the normal distribution, that is, if there are fewer values in the tails, the kurtosis measure is negative. If the distribution is flatter than the normal distribution, that is if there are more values in the tails than a corresponding normal distribution, the kurtosis measure is positive. (For more details on how Excel computes kurtosis search Help for "KURT function").

Skewness (-0.603) is a measurement of the lack of symmetry in a distribution. If there are a few extreme small values and the tail of the distribution runs off to the left we say the distribution is negatively skewed and our skewness value would be negative. If there are a few extremely large values and the tail of the distribution runs off to the right, we say the distribution is positively skewed and the skewness value would be positive. The formula for finding skewness used by Excel is different than the Pearson's Coefficient of Skewness used in the Statistical Techniques in Business and Economics textbook. (Excel computes the skewness value using the third power of the deviations from the mean. For more details on how Excel computes skewness search Help for "SKEW function").

Scatter Diagrams

When we study a single variable we refer to it as **univariate** data. When we want to look at two variables and see if they may have a relationship we refer to this as **bivariate** data. Examples of bivariate questions would be: Is there a relationship between money spent on advertising and sales? What is the relationship between age and income? Do tall parents have tall children? A **scatter diagram** is often used to visualize the relationship between two variables. To draw a scatter diagram we scale one variable along the horizontal axis (X-axis) of a graph and the other variable along the vertical axis (Y-axis). Chapter 13 will go into more details on scatter diagrams and on measuring the relationship between bivariate data. There are a couple of cautions when using scatter diagrams. First, the data must be at least interval scale. Second, be aware that the scale you use for the vertical and horizontal axis, can affect the apparent visual strength of the relationship.

Example 2. Bi-Lo Appliance Stores has outlets in several large metropolitan areas. The general sales manager plans to air a commercial for a digital camera on selected local TV stations prior to a sale starting on Saturday and ending Sunday. She plans to get the information for Saturday-Sunday digital camera sales at the various outlets and pair them with the number of times the advertisement was shown on the local TV stations. The purpose is to find whether there is a relationship between the number of times the advertisement was aired and digital camera sales. The pairings are:

Location of TV Stations	Number of Airings	Saturday-Sunday Sales ($ thousands)
Buffalo	4	15
Albany	2	8
Erie	5	21
Syracuse	6	24
Rochester	3	17

1. On a new worksheet, enter the data for the problem as shown below. Notice that the data for # of Airings is entered first since it is the independent variable.

	A	B	C
1	Location	# of Airings	Sales
2	Buffalo	4	15
3	Albany	2	8
4	Erie	5	21
5	Syracuse	6	24
6	Rochester	3	17
7			

2. Highlight **B1:C6**. From the Tool bar select ChartWizard.

3. In Step 1, under Chart type, select XY (Scatter). Under Chart sub-type, the upper left chart should be selected. Click Next.

4. In Step 2, Accept the defaults. Click Next.

5. In Step 3, at the top, the Titles tab should be selected. Click on the Chart title text box, key **Correlation Between Number of TV Ads and Sales**. Tab to the Value (X) axis text box. Key **Number of Airings**. Tab to the Value (Y) axis text box. Key **Sales (in thousands)**.

6. At the top, select the Legend tab. Click in the Show legend check box to de-select the legend. Click Finish.

The condensed scatter chart is formed.

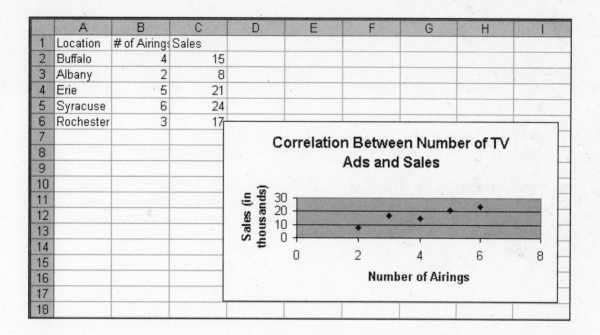

7. With the handles still on the chart, click and hold the left mouse button inside the chart. A 4-way arrow will show in the chart. As you move the chart it will show as an open box with dashed lines. With your mouse button still depressed, drag your mouse and move your chart so the left edge of the chart is in column D and the top edge of the chart is in row 2.

8. Click on the bottom handle of the chart. Drag the bottom line to row 16.

The chart is now larger and easier to read.

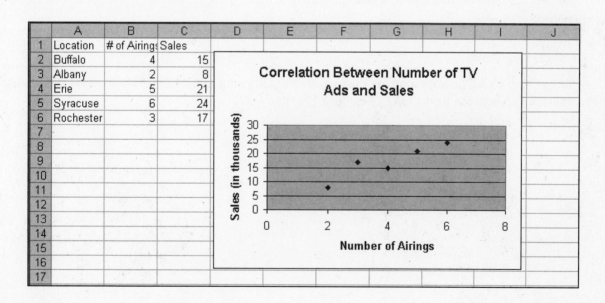

As you can see from the scatter diagram there is appositive relationship between the number of times the advertisement was aired and digital camera sales. In chapter 13 we will study the relationship between the variables.

Practice Exercises taken from textbook. (Put all related data in a single column.)

4-1. The Thomas Supply Company, Inc is a distributor of small electrical motors. As with any business, the length of time customers take to pay their invoices is important. Listed below, arranged from smallest to largest, is the time in days for a sample of The Thomas Supply Company, Inc. invoices (Textbook Problem 4-13)

13 13 13 20 26 27 31 34 34 34 34 35 35 36 37 38
41 41 41 45 47 47 47 50 51 53 54 54 56 62 37 82

Use Excel's Descriptive Statistics Output Table to find the mean, standard error, median, mode, standard deviation, sample variance, kurtosis, skewness, range, minimum, maximum, sum count, largest (2), smallest (2), and estimate quartile one, quartile two, the first decile, and the ninth decile and the 67th percentile.

4-2. Kevin Horn is the national sales manager for National Textbooks, Inc. He has a sales staff of 40 who visit college professors all over the United States. Each Saturday morning he requires his sales staff to send him a report. This report includes, among other things, the number of professors visited during the previous week. Listed below, ordered from smallest to largest, are the number of visits last week. (Textbook Problem 4-14)

38 40 41 45 48 48 50 50 51 51 52 52 53 54 55 55 55 56 56 57
59 59 59 62 62 62 63 64 65 66 66 67 67 69 69 71 77 78 79 79

Use Excel's Descriptive Statistics Output Table to find the mean, standard error, median, mode, standard deviation, sample variance, kurtosis, skewness, range, minimum, maximum, sum count, largest (2), smallest (2), and estimate quartile one, quartile two, the first decile, and the ninth decile and the 33rd percentile

4-3. Using Excel, develop a scatter diagram for the following sample data. How would you describe the relationship between the values? (Textbook Problem 4-27)

X-Value	Y-Value
10	6
8	2
9	6
11	5
13	7
11	6
10	5
7	2
7	3
11	7

4-4. An auto insurance company reported the following information regarding the age of a driver and the number of accidents reported last year. Using Excel, develop a scatter diagram for the data below and write a brief summary. (Textbook Problem 4-45)

Age	Accidents
16	4
24	2
18	5
17	4
23	0
27	1
32	1
22	3

CHAPTER

5

A SURVEY OF PROBABILITY CONCEPTS

CHAPTER GOALS

After completing this chapter, you will be able to:

1. Define and use the counting techniques to find permutations.

2. Define and use the counting techniques to find combinations.

3. Use Excel to find the number of permutations in a subset.

4. Use Excel to find the number of combinations in a subset.

Introduction

Chapter 5 of the textbook explains the principles of probability – a number between zero and one that describes the relative possibility (chance or likelihood) an event will occur. It explains the two different approaches to probability, **subjective**, and **objective**. Subjective probability is based on intuition, feelings, or judgment. Objective probability is subdivided into (1) **classical probability** and **empirical probability**. Classical or a priori is based on the assumption that the outcomes of an experiment are equally likely. That is, they are built into the experiment such as tossing a coin. When you toss a fair coin, the probability of a head is ½ or .5 and the probability of a tail is ½ or .5. Empirical, which is sometimes called relative frequency, posterior, or historical probability is based on records and past experience

If events are **mutually exclusive** they can not occur simultaneously. With one flip of a coin you get a head or a tail. **Collectively exhaustive** means that the sample space must contain all possible outcomes. If events are **independent**, one result does not influence the other result. When I flip a coin, the second flip is independent of the results of my first flip. Using the coin-flipping concept, we could say that the **compliment** of getting a head is getting a tail.

The words "**and**" and "**independent**" are used with the **multiplication rules** of probability. The **general rule of multiplication** states that the probability of events "A" and "B" which are not independent is the probability of event "A" times the probability of event "B/A." For example using a deck of fifty-two cards, the probability of being dealt four aces in a row without reshuffling would be 4/52 times 3/51 times 2/50 times 1/49. The **special rule of multiplication** states that events which are independent is the probability of event "A" times the probability of event "B." For example, the probability of being dealt four aces in a row with reshuffling would be 4/52 times 4/52 times 4/52 times 4/52.

The words "**or**" and "**mutually exclusive**" are used with the **addition rules of probability**. The **general rule of addition** states that the probability of events "A" or "B" when the events are not mutually exclusive is the probability of "A" plus the probability of "B" minus the probability of "A" and "B." For example, the probability of a king or spade in a deck of fifty-two cards would be: The probability of a king (4/52) plus the probability of a spade (13/52), minus the probability of the king of spades (1/52). The **special rule of addition** states that the probability of events "A" or "B" when the events are mutually exclusive is the probability of "A" plus the probability of "B." For example, the probability of a king or a queen is 4/52 plus 4/52.

Conditional probability is the probability of an event taking place given information that is revised. The textbook uses a tree diagram and the formula for Bayes' Theorem to explain conditional probability.

Spreadsheets using Excel would be advantageous to accomplish the arithmetic needed to solve the above problems if they were repetitious. However, when doing one or two problems a calculator is more convenient.

The formulas for the **counting techniques** of finding **combinations** and **permutations** are built into Excel. Excel, therefore, is useful to find how many subsets can be obtained from a set. In selecting the elements in the subsets, the distinction between combinations and permutations depends on whether the order of the selection makes a difference. The numbers 1, 2, and 3 are different permutations when arranged as 123 or 321 because order is important. However, 123 and 321 are the combinations of 1, 2, and 3 when order is not important. If we divide a class of 27 students into groups or teams of three, each team of three students would be a combination, because the team would be the same people regardless of the order. If we wanted to know how many ways we could park 5 cars in 21 empty parking spaces. The answer would be a permutation since order is important. If Sam's car is next to the front door that is different than if Joan's car is next to the front door.

Permutations and Combinations

When you use Excel to find permutations and combinations, the dialog box fills most of the screen. The cell that is active when you access the different functions is the cell in which the results will be displayed. Be sure to identify your work.

Example 1. Suppose there are eight machines but only three spaces on the floor of the machine shop for the machines. In how many different ways can eight machines be arranged in the three available spaces?

On a new worksheet, key the following as shown on the following page.

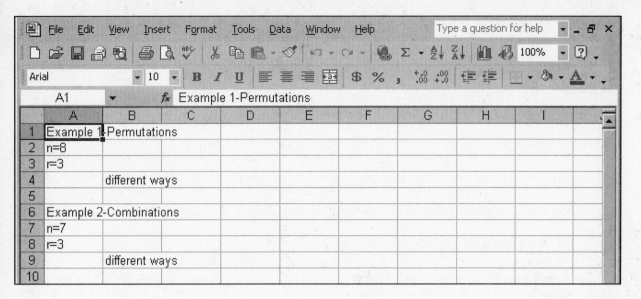

Make A4 your active cell.

1. Click on the Insert Function icon that is located at the top and to the left of the formula bar.

The Insert Function dialog box is displayed.

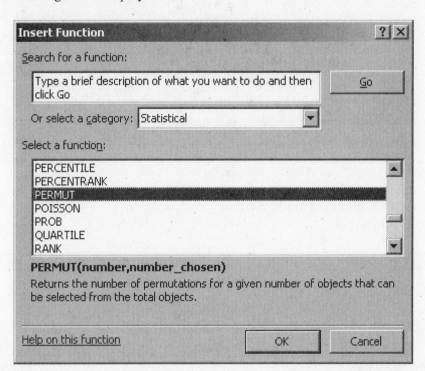

2. Click your mouse arrow on the down arrow of the Or select a category: scroll bar. Select Statistical.

3. Click your mouse arrow on the down arrow of the **Select a function:** scroll bar. Select **PERMUT.**

4. Click **OK.**

The second dialog box contains several text boxes to fill.

The ***Number*** text box is the number of objects, commonly referred to as *n*.

The ***Number_chosen*** text box is the number of objects in each permutation, commonly referred to as *r*.

5. Your cursor should be on the **Number** text box. Key **8**. Touch the **tab** key.

6. In the **Number_chosen** text box, key **3**.

As soon as you enter the number in the Number_chosen text box, the permutation shows after *Formula result =* in the lower left corner of the dialog box.

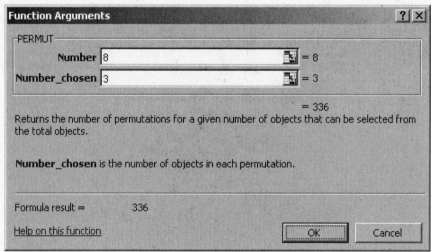

7. Click **OK.**

The permutation of 336 is displayed in cell A4.
Bold the contents of A1 and A4.

	A	B	C	D	E	F	G	H	I	
1	**Example 1-Permutations**									
2	n=8									
3	r=3									
4	336	different ways								
5										
6	Example 2 - Combinations									
7	n=7									
8	r=3									
9		different combinations								
10										

Example 2: The marketing department has been given the assignment of designing color codes for the different lines of compact discs sold by Goody Records. The three colors are to be used on each CD, but a combination of three colors used for one CD cannot be rearranged and used to identify a different CD. This means that if green, yellow, and violet were used to identify one line, then yellow, green, and violet (or any combination of these three colors) cannot be used to identify another line. How many different combinations could be created from seven colors?

On the same worksheet make A9 your active cell.

1. Click on the Insert Function icon to the left of the formula bar.

2. Click your mouse arrow on the down arrow of the Or select a category scroll bar., select Math & Trig.

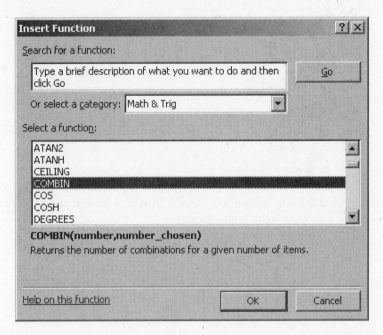

3. Click your mouse arrow on the down arrow of the Select a function: scroll bar, select COMBIN.

4. Click OK.

The second dialog box contains several text boxes to fill.

The **number** text box is the number of items commonly referred to as n.

The **number_chosen** text box is the number of objects in each combination, commonly referred to as r.

5. Your cursor should be on the number text box. Key **7**. Touch the tab key.

6. In the number_chosen text box, key **3**.

As soon as your last data is entered, the combination shows after *Formula result* = in the lower left corner of the dialog box.

    7.   Click **OK**.

The combination value of 35 is displayed in cell A9.

Bold the contents of A6 and A9.

	A	B	C	D	E	F	G	H	I	
1	**Example 1-Permutations**									
2	n=8									
3	r=3									
4	336	different ways								
5										
6	**Example 2 - Combinations**									
7	n=7									
8	r=3									
9	35	different combinations								
10										

If you wish, save your file as **permcomb**.

You can put several different problems on one worksheet. Just be sure the cell in which you want the result is the active cell when you access the Paste Function.

Practice Exercises taken from textbook.

5-1. For the daily lottery game in Illinois, participants select three numbers between 0 and 9. A number cannot be selected more than once, so a winning ticket could be, say, 307. Purchasing one ticket allows you to select one set of numbers. The winning numbers are announced on TV each night. How many different outcomes (three-digit numbers) are possible? (Textbook Problem 5-72)

5-2. A national pollster has developed 15 questions designed to rate the performance of the President of the United States. The pollster will select 10 of these questions. How many different arrangements are there for the order of the 10 questions? (Textbook Problem 5-45)

5-3. A representative of the Environmental Protection Agency (EPA) wants to select samples from 10 landfills. She has 15 landfills from which she can collect samples. How many different samples are possible? (Textbook Problem 5-44)

5-4. A puzzle in the newspaper presents a matching problem. The names of 10 U.S. presidents are listed in one column, and their vice presidents are listed in random order in the second column. The puzzle asks the reader to match each president with his vice president. If you make matches randomly, how many matches are possible? (Textbook Problem 5-83)

CHAPTER
6
DISCRETE PROBABILITY DISTRIBUTIONS

CHAPTER GOALS

After completing this chapter, you will be able to:

1. Define and use discrete probability distributions.

2. Use Excel to create discrete probability distributions.

3. Use Excel to find binomial probabilities.

4. Use Excel to find hypergeometric probabilities.

5. Use Excel to find Poisson distributions.

Introduction

Chapter 2 showed you how you can use Excel to graphically portray data in pie charts, bar charts, histograms, line charts, etc. Chapter 3 emphasized descriptive statistics with measurements of central tendency and dispersion. That chapter was concerned with descriptive statistics, describing something that had already occurred.

Chapter 5 introduced us to probability concepts. Chapter 6 turns to the second facet of statistics, that is, computing the chance or probability that something *will* occur. This facet of statistics is referred to as **inferential statistics** or **statistical inference.**

Statistical inference makes a statement about a population based on a sample taken from that population. Any time we use statistical inferences there is a chance of making an error or being wrong. *Probability theory* scientifically evaluates the risks involved in making these inferences. Probability theory allows the decision maker with only limited information to analyze the risks and minimize the gamble inherent in such things as marketing a new product or accepting a shipment containing defects.

This chapter will show how you can use Excel to find three different **discrete distributions**: the **binomial distribution,** the **hypergeometric distribution** and the **Poisson distribution** to model and analyze real-world processes. These distributions involve discrete random variables, variables that can assume only certain clearly separated values resulting from counts of an item of interest. The number of rooms in a house, the number of people in a room, and the number of pop cans purchased for a party are all discrete random variables. These are different from **continuous distributions** which deal with continuous random variables that can assume any value in an interval. Such measurements as width of a room, the height of a person, and the amount of pop in a can of Coke are all examples of continuous random variables. In the next chapter we will discuss continuous distributions.

Here are a few examples of discrete probability distributions and how they are used.

Binomial Distribution

When you use Excel to find various statistical functions, the dialog box fills most of the screen. The cell that is active when you access the different functions is the cell in which the result will be displayed. On a new worksheet, key the following as shown:

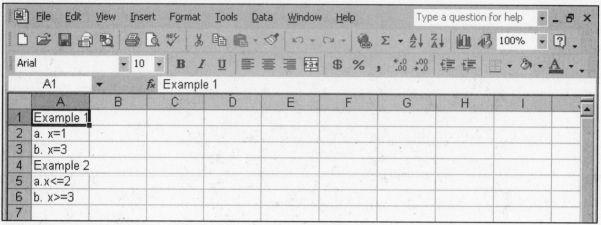

Make B2 your active cell.

To use the binomial distribution function of Excel, do the following:

1. Click on the Insert Function icon to the left of the formula bar.

The Insert Function dialog box is displayed.

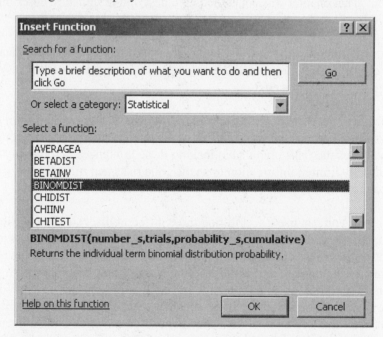

2. Click your mouse arrow on the down arrow of the Or select a category: scroll bar. Select Statistical.

3. From the Select a function: list box, select BINOMDIST. Click on OK.

The BINOMDIST dialog box contains several text boxes to fill.

The *Number_s* text box is for the number of observed successes, commonly referred to as x.

The *Trials* text box is for the number of trials, commonly referred to as n.

The *Probability_s* text box is for the probability of success on each trial, commonly referred to as π.

The *Cumulative* text box is used to indicate whether x, the number of observed successes, is cumulative or not cumulative. You would key 1 for true if you want the cumulative probability that includes the numbers up to and including the value of x. You would key 0 for false (or not cumulative) if x is the number of observed successes only.

You will use the step 2 dialog box to solve the following problem:

Example 1. In a binomial distribution, n=5 and π = .20, determine the following probabilities:
(a) $x = 1$, (b) $x = 3$.

    1. Your cursor should be on the Numbers_s text box. Key **1**. Touch the tab key.

    2. In the Trials text box, key **5**. Touch the tab key.

    3. In the Probability_s text box, key **.20** . Touch the tab key.

    4. In the Cumulative text box, since you want exactly 1 observed success, key **0** for false (not cumulative).

As soon as you enter the number in the Cumulative text box, the probability shows after the Formula result = in the lower left corner of the dialog box.

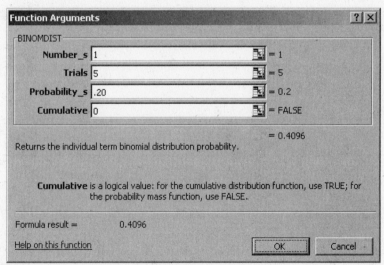

    5. Click OK.
The probability value of .4096 is displayed in cell B2.

To complete part b of example 1, make B3 your active cell. Repeat steps 1-9 but key **3** for the value of *x* in the **Number_s** text box. You should get a probability value of .0512.

Make cell B5 your active cell.

You will use the BINOMDIST function to solve the following problem.

Example 2. In a binomial distribution, where n = 8 and = .30, determine the following probabilities: (a) *x* 2, (b) *x* 3.

   1. Follow steps 1 - 4 from the previous exercise.

   2. Your cursor should be in the **number_s** text box. Key **2**. Touch the **tab** key.

   3. In the **trials** text box, key **8**. Touch the **tab** key.

   4. In the **probability_s** text box, key **.30**. Touch the **tab** key.

   5. Your cursor should be in the **cumulative** text box, since you want to select cumulative (0 through 2 inclusive), key **1** for true.

   6. Click **OK**.

The probability value of .551774 is now displayed in cell B5.

Make cell B6 your active cell. Key in the formula =**1-B5**. Touch the <Enter> key. The value .448226, which is the compliment of *x* 2, is displayed. This is the answer to part (b) of Example 2.

	A	B	C	D	E	F	G	H	I	
1	Example1									
2	a. x=1	0.4096								
3	b. x=3	0.0512								
4	Example2									
5	a. x<=2	0.551774								
6	b. x>=3	0.448226								
7										

If you wanted to know the probability for *x* being < 2, you would use *x* = 1 in the **Number_s** text box and 1 (or true) for the **Cumulative** text box. This would give you the probabilities for 0 and 1 inclusive, which is less than 2. You can use the BINOMDIST function and the complement of the probability (subtracted from 1) to solve binomial distributions.

Click your mouse arrow on the **Print** button to print your first two examples.

Example 3. Assume a binomial distribution where n = 5 and $\not{a}$ = .30. List the probabilities of a success for values of *x* from 0 to 5.

      1. Starting with cell D1, key in the information for Example 3 as shown below.

	A	B	C	D	E	F	G	H	I	
1	Example1			Example3						
2	a. x=1	0.4096			probability					
3	b. x=3	0.0512		x	of occurrence					
4	Example2			0						
5	a. x<=2	0.551774		1						
6	b. x>=3	0.448226		2						
7				3						
8				4						
9				5						
10										

      2. Make cell E4 your active cell.

      3. Select the binomial distribution function as shown earlier. Your cursor should be on the Numbers_s text box. Key **D4**. Touch the tab key.

      4. In the Trials text box, key **5**. Touch the tab key.

      5. In the Probability_s text box, key **.30**. Touch the tab key.

      6. In the Cumulative text box, key **0**. Click on OK.

The probability of .16807 shows in cell E4. Place your mouse arrow on the lower right handle of cell E4. It will change to a thick black plus sign. Click, hold and drag the cursor to cell E9. The probability amounts have been automatically filled in. From the Tool bar, click on the AutoSum icon. Note that the probabilities are collectively exhaustive. That is, they add up to 1 or 100%.

	A	B	C	D	E	F	G	H	I	
1	Example1			Example3						
2	a. x=1	0.4096			probability					
3	b. x=3	0.0512		x	of occurrence					
4	Example2			0	0.16807					
5	a. x<=2	0.551774		1	0.36015					
6	b. x>=3	0.448226		2	0.3087					
7				3	0.1323					
8				4	0.02835					
9				5	0.00243					
10					1					
11										

As Example 3 shows, you can use Excel to create tables. Make sure you have a cell reference in the Number_s text box instead of a value.

Hypergeometric Distribution

Example 4.   Suppose that a population consists of 10 items, 6 of which are defective. A sample of 3 items is selected. What is the probability that exactly 2 items are defective?

On the same worksheet, in cell A11 key **Example 4**. In A12 key **x=2**. Make B12 your active cell.

To use the hypergeometric distribution function of Excel, do the following.

1. Click on the Insert Function icon to the left of the formula bar.

2. From the Or select a category: list box, select Statistical.

3. Click your mouse arrow on the down arrow of the Select a function: scroll bar. Select HYPGEOMDIST.

4. Click OK.

The HYPGEOMDIST dialog box contains several text boxes to fill.

The *Sample_s* text box is for the number of successes of interest, commonly referred to as x.

The *Number_s* sample text box is for the size of the sample or the number of trials, commonly referred to as n.

The *Population_s* text box is for the number of successes in the population, commonly referred to as S.

The *Number_population* text box is for the size of the population, commonly referred to as N.

You will use the step 2 dialog box to continue this example.

5. Your cursor should be on the Sample_s text box. Key **2**. Touch the tab key.

6. In the Number_s sample text box, key **3**. Touch the tab key.

7. In the Population_s text box, key **6**. Touch the tab key.

8. In the Number_population text box, key **10**.

As soon as your last data is entered, the probability shows after the Formula result = in the lower left corner of the dialog box.

9. Click OK.

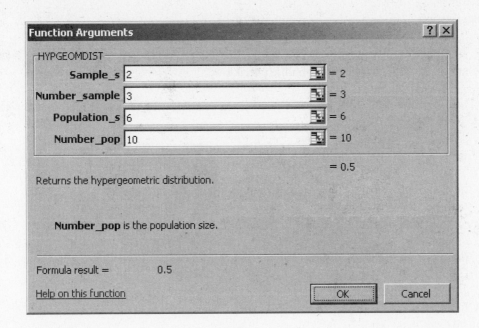

The probability value of .5 is now displayed in cell B12.

	A	B	C	D	E	F	G	H	I
1	Example1			Example3					
2	a. x=1	0.4096			probability				
3	b. x=3	0.0512		x	of occurrence				
4	Example2			0	0.16807				
5	a. x<=2	0.551774		1	0.36015				
6	b. x>=3	0.448226		2	0.3087				
7				3	0.1323				
8				4	0.02835				
9				5	0.00243				
10					1				
11	Example4								
12	x=2	0.5							
13									

Poisson Distribution

Example 5. In a Poisson distribution $\cup$ = 4, (a) what is the probability that x = 2? (b) what is the probability that x   2? (c) what is the probability that x > 2?

In cell D11 key **Example 5**. In Cell D12 key **a**. **x=2** In cell D13 key **b. x<=2**. In cell D14 key **c. x>2**. Make cell E12 your active cell.

To use the Poisson distribution function of Excel, do the following:

1. Click on the Insert Function icon to the left of the formula bar.

2. From the Or select a category: list box, select Statistical.

3. Click your mouse arrow on the down arrow of the Select a function: scroll bar. Select POISSON.

4. Click OK.

Step 2 of the POISSON dialog box contains several text boxes to fill.

The *X* text box is for the number of occurrences (successes).

The *Mean* text box is for the arithmetic mean number of occurrences (successes) in a particular interval of time, commonly referred to as (mu) $\cup$.

The *Cumulative* text box is used to indicate whether *X*, the number of occurrences (successes) is cumulative or not cumulative. You would key 1 for true (cumulative) or 0 for false (not cumulative).

You will use the step 2 dialog box to continue this example.

5. Your cursor should be in the *X* text box. Key **2**. Touch the tab key.

6. In the Mean text box, key **4**. Touch the tab key.

7. In the Cumulative text box, key **0**.

8. Click OK.

The probability of .146525 is now displayed in cell E12.

Make E13 your active cell. Repeat steps 1 – 8 but key **1** in the cumulative text box. You should get a probability of .238103. Make cell E14 your active cell. Key =**1-E13**. Touch the <Enter> key. The value .761897 is displayed, which is the compliment of x <=2. This is the answer to part (c) of Example 5.

	A	B	C	D	E	F	G	H	I
1	Example1			Example3					
2	a. x=1	0.4096			probability				
3	b. x=3	0.0512		x	of occurrence				
4	Example2			0	0.16807				
5	a. x<=2	0.551774		1	0.36015				
6	b. x>=3	0.448226		2	0.3087				
7				3	0.1323				
8				4	0.02835				
9				5	0.00243				
10					1				
11	Example4			Example5					
12	x=2	0.5		a. x=2	0.146525				
13				b. x<=2	0.238103				
14				c. x>2	0.761897				
15									

Print Examples 1 through 5 if you wish. Close your worksheet.

Use discrete distributions to solve the following problems. Be sure to identify your outcome on the worksheet. Also remember that the cell that is active when you work the exercises is the cell in which the results will be displayed.

Practice Exercises taken from textbook.

6-1 An American Society of Investors survey found 30 percent of individual investors have used a discount broker. In a random sample of nine individuals, what is the probability: (Textbook Problem 6-13)
a. Exactly two of the sampled individuals have used a discount broker.
b. Exactly four of them used a discount broker.
c. None of them used a discount broker.

6-2. A Tamiami shearing machine is producing 10 percent defective pieces, which is abnormally high. The quality-control engineer has been checking the output by almost continuous sampling since the abnormal condition began. What is the probability that in a sample of 10 pieces: (Textbook Problem 6-45)

a. Exactly 5 will be defective?
b. 5 or more will be defective?

6-3. In a binomial distribution n = 12 and π = .60. Find the probabilities. (Textbook Problem 6-20)

a. $x = 5$
b. x 5.
c. x 6.

6-4. A manufacturer of window frames knows from long experience that 5 percent of the production will have some type of minor defect that will require an adjustment. What is the probability that in a sample of 20 window frames: (Textbook Problem 6-22)

a. None will need adjustment?
b. At least 1 will need adjustment?
c. More than 2 will need adjustment?

6-5. A population consists of 15 items, 10 of which are acceptable. In a sample of 4 items what is the probability that exactly 3 are acceptable? Assume the samples are drawn without replacements. (Textbook Problem 6-26)

6-6. The Computer Systems Department has eight faculty, six of whom are tenured. Dr. Vonder, the chairman, wants to establish a committee of three department faculty members to review the curriculum. If she selects the committee at random: (Textbook Problem 6-28)

a. What is the probability all members of the committee are tenured?
b. What is the probability that at least one member is not tenured? (Hint: For this question use the complement rule.)

6-7. Professor Jon Hammer has a pool of 15 multiple-choice questions regarding probability distributions. Four of these questions involve the hypergeometric distribution. What is the probability at least 1 of these hypergeometric questions will appear on the 5 question quiz on Monday? (Textbook Problem 6-30)

6-8. Automobiles arrive at the Elkhart exit of the Indiana Toll Road at the rate of two per minute. The distribution of arrivals approximates a Poisson distribution. (Textbook Problem 6-34)

a. What is the probability that no automobiles arrive in a particular minute?
b. What is the probability that at least one automobile arrives during a particular minute?

6-9. Textbook authors and publishers work very hard to minimize the number of errors in a text. However, some errors are unavoidable. Mr. J. A. Carmen, statistics editor, reports that the mean number of errors per chapter is 0.8. What is the probability that there are less than 2 errors in a particular chapter? (Textbook Problem 6-36)

6-10. Suppose 1.5 percent of the antennas on new Nokia cell phones are defective. For a random sample of 200 antennas, find the probability that: (Textbook Problem 6-62)

a. None of the antennas are defective.
b. Three or more of the antennas are defective.

CHAPTER
7
CONTINUOUS PROBABILITY DISTRIBUTIONS

CHAPTER GOALS

After completing this chapter, you will be able to:

1. Define and use normal probability distributions.

2. Use Excel to create a normal probability distribution.

3. Use Excel and the standard normal distribution to determine the probability that an observation will be above or below a value.

4. Use Excel and the standard normal distribution to determine the probability that an observation will lie between two points.

5. Use Excel and the standard normal distribution to find the value of an observation when the percent above or below the observation is given.

Introduction

Chapter 6 dealt with discrete probability distributions. This chapter will continue the study of probability distributions by examining a very important continuous probability distribution, the **normal probability distribution.** As noted in the preceding chapter, a continuous random variable is one that can assume an infinite number of possible values within a specified range. It usually results from measuring something, such as the amount of gasoline in a tank. The number of gallons might be 11.0 gallons, 11.1 gallons, 11.12 gallons, and so on, depending on the accuracy of the measurement. Other continuous variables include weights, time, temperature, length, width, etc. Many measurements tend to follow a "normal" pattern. The weights of the beef patties to make McDonald's Quarter Pounder, the average heights of American men, and the amount of Pepsi in a can are all examples of continuous random variables that tend to be normally distributed. A normal probability distribution is bell-shaped, symmetrical and asymptotic.

Areas Under the Normal Curve

When you use your text to compute the area under a curve, the given area is to the left or right of the *mean*. When using Excel to compute the normal cumulative distribution, the area is cumulative from the *left side* of the curve. Therefore if you want to compute an area between *x* and the mean, you will compute the difference between the given area and .5 (half the area under the curve). In this exercise we will create several worksheet templates that can be used for a variety of purposes.

Example 1. Creating a worksheet (template) to use for finding normal probability distributions.

    1. On a new worksheet enter the cell contents as shown below.

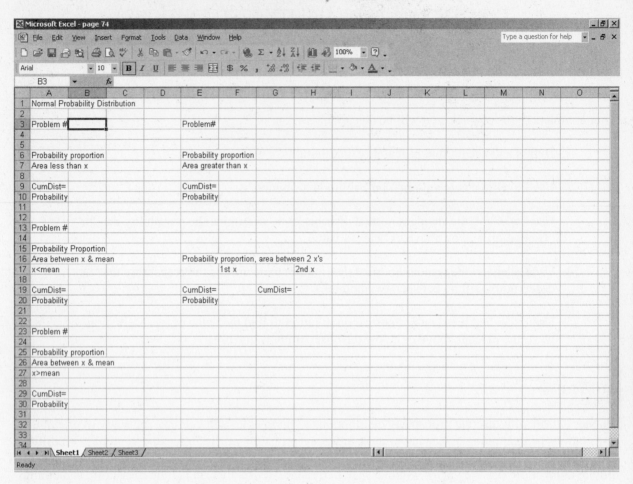

Cells A3:B10 will be used for finding the area less than x. Since Excel computes this area automatically, no other computations are needed.

    2. In cell B20, key **=.5-B19**

Cells A13:B20 will be used when the area is between x and the mean, and x is less than the mean. Since Excel computes only the area less than x, that value must be subtracted from .5 (half the area under the curve) to find the area in between.

    3. In cell B30, key **=B29-.5**

Cells A23:B30 will be used when the area is between x and the mean, and x is greater than the mean. Since Excel computes only the area less than x, .5 (half the area under the curve) must be subtracted from that value.

    4. In cell F10, key **=1-F9**

Cells E3:F10 will be used when the area is more than x. Since Excel computes only the area less than x, that value must be subtracted from 1 (the total area under the curve.)

   5. In cell F20, key =**H19-F19**

Cells E13:H20 will be used when the area is between two values of x. The smaller value of x is used as the 1st number and the larger value of x as the 2nd number, then the two areas are subtracted.

When you are finished with the formulas, the cell contents of your worksheet should look as shown below. Remember, to switch to formula view, hold the control key down while tapping the tilde key. You may have to adjust the column width to be able to view the entire formula.

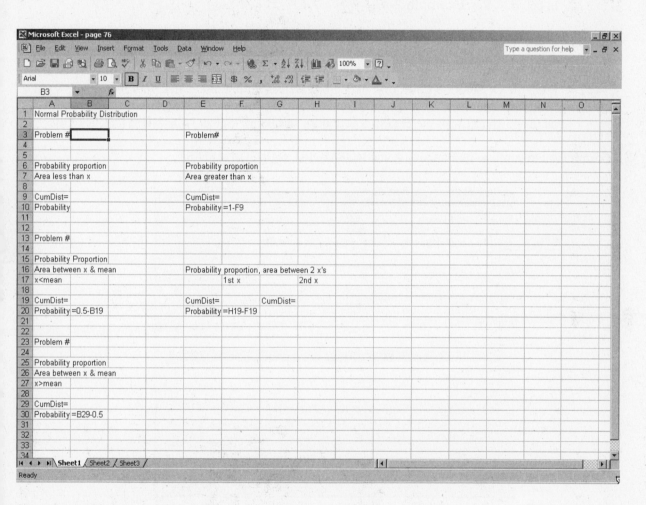

Save your worksheet as **normprbd**. (If needed, refer to Chapter 1 on how to save.)

When you use Excel's Normal Distribution function, the cell that is active is the cell in which the results will be displayed. Before you choose the function always make sure your active cell is the cell to the right of the cell containing the label CumDist=.

Example 2. The employees of Cartwright Manufacturing are awarded efficiency ratings. The distribution of the ratings approximates a normal distribution. The mean is 400, the standard deviation 50. (a) What is the area under the normal curve between 400 and 482? (b) What is the area under the normal curve for ratings greater than 482? (c) What is the area under the normal curve for ratings greater than 500?

    1. If it is not already open, retrieve file **normprbd**.

Since part a is for an area between *x* and the mean, and *x* is greater than the mean, you will use cells A23:B30.

    2. In cell B23, key **Example 2-a**.

    3. Make B29 your active cell since that is where you want the results to be displayed. Click on the Insert Function icon to the left of the formula bar.

    4. From the Or select a category: dialog box, select Statistical. Click your mouse arrow on the down arrow of the Select a function: scroll bar. Select NORMDIST. Click OK.

Be careful not to confuse the Function name NORMDIST with NORMSDIST.

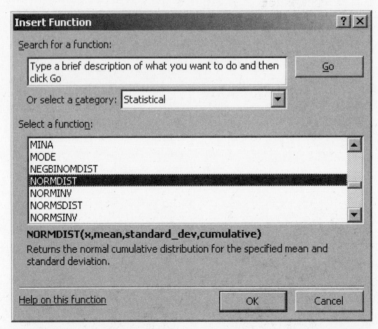

The dialog box for NORMDIST is displayed.

    5. The cursor should be on the X text box. Key **482**. Touch the tab key.

    6. In the Mean text box, key **400**. Touch the tab key.

    7. In the Standard_dev text box, key **50**. Touch the tab key.

8. In the Cumulative text box, key **1** for true. (The cumulative text box will always contain 1) Click OK.

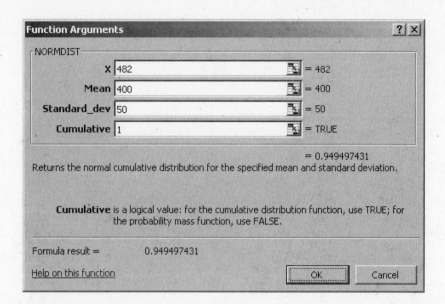

The cumulative distribution is displayed in A29 and the probability (area) is displayed in A20. The area between 400 and 482 is .449497.

9. Make B23 your active cell. From the Tool bar, select the Bold icon.

10. Make B30 your active cell. From the Tool bar, select the Bold icon.

This makes the answer easier to associate with the problem.

If you were to key 0 in the cumulative text box, the resulting value would be the height of the normal density function. If you were to plot the bell curve, this height would be useful for finding the value at which the curve peaks.

Since part b of Example 2 is for an area greater than x you will use cells E3:F10.

11. In cell F3, key **Example 2-b**.

12. Make F9 your active cell since you want the results to be displayed in this cell. Click on the Insert Function icon.

13. From the Or select a category: dialog box, select Statistical. Click your mouse arrow on the down arrow of the Select a function: scroll bar. Select NORMDIST. Click OK.

You will enter the same data as before.

14. The cursor should be on the X text box. Key **482**. Touch the tab key.

15. In the Mean text box, key **400**. Touch the tab key.

16. In the Standard_dev text box, key **50**. Touch the tab key.

17. In the Cumulative text box, key **1**. Click OK.

The cumulative distribution is displayed in F9, and the probability (area) is displayed in F10. The area greater than 482 is .050503.

18. Bold the contents of cells F3 and F10.

Since part c of Example 2 also is for an area greater than x, you will use cells E6:F10 again. Since you don't need the cell contents for the area less than x, you will replace those cells.

19. Highlight **A6:B10**. Touch the <Delete> key.

20. Highlight **E6:F10**. From the Tool bar, select the Copy button.

21. Make A6 your active cell. From the Tool bar, select the Paste button. Touch the <Enter> key.

The data for Example 2-b is repeated. You will replace the cells with data from Example 2-c.

22. In B3, key **Example 2-c**.

23. Make B9 your active cell. Click on the Insert Function icon.

The completed dialog box from Example 2-b is displayed. Since everything is the same except the data for the x text box, you will change just that data.

24. Click your mouse arrow on the x text box. Use the <Back Space> key to remove the data of 482. Key **500**. Click OK.

25. Bold the contents of B3.

	A	B	C	D	E	F	G	H	I	
1	Normal Probability Distribution									
2										
3	Problem #	**Example 2-c**			Problem #	**Example 2-b**				
4										
5										
6	Probability proportion				Probability proportion					
7	Area greater than x				Area greater than x					
8										
9	CumDist=	0.97725			CumDist=	0.949497				
10	Probability	**0.02275**			Probability	**0.050503**				
11										
12										
13	Problem #				Problem #					
14										
15	Probability Proportion									
16	Area between x & mean				Probability proportion, area between 2 x's					
17	x<mean					1st x		2nd x		
18										
19	CumDist=				CumDist=		CumDist=			
20	Probability	0.5			Probability	0				
21										
22										
23	Problem #	**Example 2-a**								
24										
25	Probability proportion									
26	Area between x & mean									
27	x>mean									
28										
29	CumDist=	0.949497								
30	Probability	**0.449497**								
31										

Finding the Value of the Observation X when the Percent Above or Below the Observation is Given.

Excel also has a function to find the value of *x* when you know the probability, mean, and standard deviation.

Example 3. An analysis of the final test scores for a computer programming seminar revealed that they approximate a normal curve with a mean of 75, and a standard deviation of 8. The instructor wants to award the grade of A to the upper 10 percent of the test grades. What is the dividing point between an A and a B grade?

Since he wants the upper 10 percent, that means there will be 90 percent lower than that, so you will use .90 as the probability. Again, the cell that is active is the cell in which the results will be displayed.

1. On the same worksheet, in E23, key **Example 3**.

2. Make E24 your active cell. Click on the Insert Function icon.

3. From the Or select a <u>c</u>ategory: dialog box, select Statistical. Click your mouse arrow on the down arrow of the Select a functio<u>n</u>: scroll bar. Select NORMINV. Click OK.

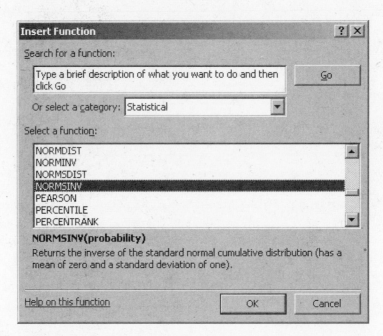

The dialog box for NORMINV is similar to the one for NORMDIST.

4. The cursor should be on the Probability text box. Key **.90**. Touch the tab key.

5. In the Mean text box, key **75**. Touch the tab key.

6. In the Standard_dev text box, key **8**. Click OK.

Function Arguments ?|X|

NORMINV

Probability	.90		= 0.9
Mean	75		= 75
Standard_dev	8		= 8

= 85.25241551

Returns the inverse of the normal cumulative distribution for the specified mean and standard deviation.

Standard_dev is the standard deviation of the distribution, a positive number.

Formula result =   85.25241551

Help on this function   OK   Cancel

The result of 85.25241 is displayed. Therefore a test score of 85 is the dividing grade between an A and a B.

	A	B	C	D	E	F	G	H	I
1	Normal Probability Distribution								
2									
3	Problem #	**Example 2-c**			Problem #	**Example 2-b**			
4									
5									
6	Probability proportion				Probability proportion				
7	Area greater than x				Area greater than x				
8									
9	CumDist=	0.97725			CumDist=	0.949497			
10	Probability	**0.02275**			Probability	**0.050503**			
11									
12									
13	Problem #				Problem #				
14									
15	Probability Proportion								
16	Area between x & mean				Probability proportion, area between 2 x's				
17	x<mean					1st x		2nd x	
18									
19	CumDist=				CumDist=		CumDist=		
20	Probability	0.5			Probability	0			
21									
22									
23	Problem #	**Example 2-a**			**Example 3**				
24					**85.25241**				
25	Probability proportion								
26	Area between x & mean								
27	x>mean								
28									
29	CumDist=	0.949497							
30	Probability	**0.449497**							
31									

Chapter 7

Practice Exercises taken from textbook.

7-1. A normal population has a mean of 20.0 and a standard deviation of 4.0. (Textbook Problem 7-11)

a. What proportion of the population is between 20.0 and 25.0?
b. What proportion of the population is less than 18.0?

7-2. The amounts of money requested in home loan applications at Down River Federal Savings are approximately normally distributed with a mean of $70,000 and a standard deviation of $20,000. A loan application is received this morning. What is the probability that: (Textbook Problem 7-18)

a. The amount requested is $80,000 or more?
b. The amount requested is between $65,000 and $80,000?
c. The amount requested is $65,000 or more?

7-3. The accounting department at Weston Materials Inc., a national manufacturer of unattached garages, reports that it takes two construction workers a mean of 32 hours and a standard deviation of 2 hours to erect the Red Barn model. Assume the assembly times follow the normal distribution.
(Textbook Problem 7-38)

a. What percent of the garages take between 32 hours and 34 hours to erect?
b. What percent of the garages take between 29 hours and 34 hours to erect?
c. What percent of the garages take 28.7 hours or less to erect?
d. Of the garages, 5 percent take how many hours or more to erect?

7-4. The annual commissions earned by sales representatives of the Machine Products Inc., a manufacturer of light machinery, follow the normal distribution. The mean yearly amount earned is $40,000 and the standard deviation is $5000. (Textbook Problem 7-42)

a. What percent of the sales representatives earn more than $42,000 per year?
b. What percent of the sales representatives earn between $32,000 and $42,000?
c. What percent of the sales representatives earn between $32,000 and $35,000?
d. The sales manages wants to award the sales representatives who earn the largest commissions a bonus of $1,000. He can award a bonus to 20 percent of the representatives. What is the cutoff point between those who earn a bonus and those who do not?

7-5. Fast Service Truck Lines uses the Ford Super Duty F-750 exclusively. Management made a study of maintenance costs and determined the number of miles traveled during the year followed the normal distribution. The mean of the distribution was 60,000 miles and the standard deviation was 2,000 miles. (Textbook Problem 7-46)

a. What percent of the Ford Super Duty F-750s logged 65,200 miles or more?
b. What percent of the trucks log more than 57,060 miles but less than 58,280 miles?
c. How many of the Fords traveled 62,000 miles or less during the year?

7-6. In establishing warranties on HDTV sets the manufacturer wants to set the limits so that few will need repair at manufacturer expense. On the other hand, the warranty period must be long enough to make the purchase attractive to the buyer. For a new HDTV the mean number of months until repairs are needed is 36.84 with a standard deviation of 3.34 months. Where should the warranty limits be set so that only 10 percent of the HDTVs need repairs at the manufacturer's expense? (Textbook Problem 7-60)

CHAPTER
8
SAMPLING METHODS AND THE CENTRAL LIMIT THEOREM

CHAPTER GOALS

After completing this chapter, you will be able to:

1. Use Excel to show that means of small samples have more dispersion or scatter than the means of large samples.

2. Define and construct a sampling distribution of sample means.

3. Use Excel to illustrate the central limit theorem.

Introduction

The law of large numbers tells us that a large sample tends to give a better approximation of the population parameter than a small sample. This reflects a simple notion supported by common sense: In only a few trials, results can be very different, but in a large sample, results tend to be fairly stable and consistent. For example it would not be unusual to get 3 heads when flipping a fair coin 3 times, but it would be very unusual to get 300 heads when flipping a fair coin 300 times. This notion is widely used by insurance companies to estimate the expected amount of claims they will pay in any one year. It is used by government to estimate tax collections. It tells gambling casinos that when the odds favor the house, even a little bit, if they can induce enough people to gamble long enough, the house will win.

The central limit theorem states that when sampling from a normal, a uniform, or even a skewed distribution, the means of the samples will be approximately normally distributed if a sufficient number of samples are taken. The following examples will show you how you can use Excel to work with sampling and sampling distributions.

Sampling From a Normal Population

Example 1. Birth weight of a newborn is a major concern for all new parents. Nationally, the 50th percentile birth weight of children born at full term (40 weeks) is 7.04 pounds. That is, the average or "normal" birth weight of a full term baby is 7.04 pounds. From a random sample of 237 full term babies born at Community Hospital, their mean weight was 7.04 with a standard deviation of .42. To illustrate the law of large numbers from this sample of birth weights, you will:

a. Generate a random frequency distribution of weights.
b. From the frequency distribution, select two small samples and two large samples, and compare the means and standard deviations.
c. Construct histograms using a very small sampling distribution of sample means and a larger sampling distribution of sample means.

a. Generating a Random Distribution

1. On a new worksheet enter the data as shown below.

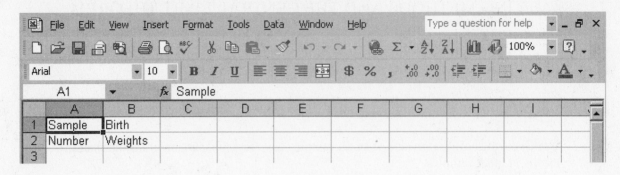

2. In A3, key **1**. Touch the <Enter> key.

3. Make A3 your active cell. From the Menu bar, select Edit. Select Fill. Select Series. From the Series dialog box, select Series in Columns. Select Type Linear. In the Step Value text box, key **1**. In the Stop Value text box, key **237**. Click OK.

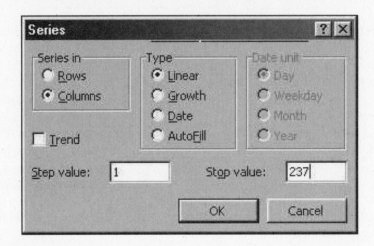

This enters the number 1-237 in A3:A239.

4. In B3, key =**NORMINV(RAND(),7.04,.42)**. Press <Enter>.

This generates a random number with a mean of 7.04 and a standard deviation of .42.

5. Make B3 your active cell. Place your mouse arrow on the lower right handle of B3. Make sure you have a thick, black plus sign. Click your left mouse button twice, rapidly.

This automatically fills the cells in B4:B239 with random numbers. Touch the F9 (re-calculate) function key on your keyboard. Notice how the random birth weights change each time. Each time you perform a new procedure, the random values change. You need to save the generated numbers so you can select random numbers from them. Your worksheet will look different from the examples that follow.

6. Highlight **A1:B239**. As you drag your mouse pointer below the worksheet it will highlight the lower rows. From the Tool bar, select the <u>C</u>opy icon.

7. From the Menu bar, select <u>F</u>ile. Select <u>C</u>lose. Select <u>N</u>o for Save changes. Select <u>Y</u>es for Save large Clipboard.

8. From the Menu bar, select <u>F</u>ile. Select <u>N</u>ew. Make A1 your active cell. From the Tool bar, select the <u>P</u>aste icon. Your random numbers should now stay as a population from which to take samples.

b. Sample Sizes and Comparisons

1. In E1:H2, enter the contents as shown below.

	A	B	C	D	E	F	G	H	I
1	Sample	Birth			Sample	Sample	Sample	Sample	
2	Number	Weights			of 3	of 3	of 30	of 30	
3	1	7.403472							
4	2	7.337615							
5	3	6.692735							
6	4	6.8831							
7	5	6.934702							
8	6	7.167506							
9	7	6.587278							
10	8	6.959932							
11	9	6.79725							
12	10	6.684729							

From the Menu bar, select <u>T</u>ools. If <u>D</u>ata Analysis does not appear, select <u>A</u>dd-Ins. Select Analysis ToolPak. Click OK.

2. From the Menu bar, select <u>T</u>ools. Select <u>D</u>ata Analysis. Place your mouse arrow on the down arrow of the side scroll bar. Select Sampling. Click OK.

The Sampling dialog box appears.

3. Your cursor should be in the text box for <u>I</u>nput Range. Key **B3:B239**

4. Select the button for <u>R</u>andom. In the Number of Samples text box, key **3**. Select the button for <u>O</u>utput Range. In the <u>O</u>utput Range text box, key **E3**. Click OK.

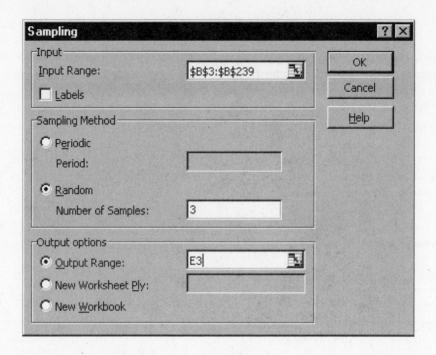

From the random weights in B3:B239, 3 were selected.

5. From the Menu bar, select Tools. Select Data Analysis. Select Sampling. Click OK.

6. Leave the Input Range as **B3:B239**. Leave the Number of Samples as **3**. In the text box for Output Range, replace the contents with **F3.** Click OK.

From the random weights in B3:B239, 3 more were selected.

7. In D6:D7, key **Mean** and **StdDev**, respectively.

8. In E6, key =**Average(E3:E5)**

9. In E7, key =**STDEV(E3:E5)**

10. Highlight **E6:E7**. Drag the lower right handle of E7 to F7.

	A	B	C	D	E	F	G	H	I
1	Sample	Weights			Sample	Sample	Sample	Sample	
2	Number	Weights			of 3	of 3	of 30	of 30	
3	1	7.403472			6.845856	7.04544			
4	2	7.337615			6.758911	6.922607			
5	3	6.692735			6.728874	7.45883			
6	4	6.8831		Mean	6.77788	7.142292			
7	5	6.934702		StdDev	0.060754	0.280925			
8	6	7.167506							
9	7	6.587278							
10	8	6.959932							
11	9	6.79725							
12	10	6.684729							

This computes the mean and standard deviation of the two samples of 3.

11. From the Menu bar, select Tools. Select Data Analysis. Select Sampling. Click OK.

12. Leave the Input Range as **B3:B239**. In the Number of Samples text box, key **30.** In the Output Range text box, key **G3**. Click OK.

From the random weights in B3:B239, 30 were selected.

13. From the Menu bar, select Tools. Select Data Analysis. Select Sampling. Click OK.

14. Leave the Input Range as **B3:B239**. Leave the Number of Samples as **30**. In the Output Range text box, key **H3**. Click OK

From the random weights in B3:B239, 30 more were selected.

15. In F33:F34, key **Mean** and **StdDev**, respectively.

16. In G33, key =**AVERAGE(G3:G32)**

17. In G34, key =**STDEV(G3:G32)**

18. Highlight **G33:G34**. Drag the lower right handle of G34 to H34.

This computes the mean and standard deviation of the two samples of 30.

19. Highlight **A9:A30**. (Column A will stop at Sample Number 28). From the Menu bar, select Format. Select Row. Select Hide.

This hides rows 9-30 and brings your mean and standard deviation of all 4 samples closer together so you can compare them.

	A	B	C	D	E	F	G	H	I
1	Sample	Birth			Sample	Sample	Sample	Sample	
2	Number	Weights			of 3	of 3	of 30	of 30	
3	1	7.403472			6.845856	7.04544	7.290466	6.476734	
4	2	7.337615			6.758911	6.922607	6.952859	7.098922	
5	3	6.692735			6.728874	7.45883	7.085119	7.012676	
6	4	6.8831		Mean	6.77788	7.142292	6.771342	7.255937	
7	5	6.934702		StdDev	0.060754	0.280925	6.119746	7.678632	
8	6	7.167506					6.393192	7.069464	
31	29	7.161848					7.067572	7.325329	
32	30	7.188481					7.316917	6.744359	
33	31	7.052134				Mean	7.026196	7.051699	
34	32	7.559373				StdDev	0.479805	0.376885	
35	33	6.925036							
36	34	7.038894							
37									

20. In C36:C37, key **% of diff mean** and **% of diff StdDev**, respectively.

21. In H36:H37, key **% of diff mean** and **% of diff StdDev**, respectively.

22. In E36, key =**ABS(E6-F6)/E6**

This computes the absolute (positive) value of the percent of difference between the two means.

23. In E37, key =**ABS(E7-F7)/E7**

24. In G36, key =**ABS(G33-H33)/G33**

25. In G37, key =**ABS(G34-H34)/G34**

This allows you to compare the means and standard deviations.

	A	B	C	D	E	F	G	H	I	
1	Sample	Birth			Sample	Sample	Sample	Sample		
2	Number	Weights			of 3	of 3	of 30	of 30		
3	1	7.403472			6.845856	7.04544	7.290466	6.476734		
4	2	7.337615			6.758911	6.922607	6.952859	7.098922		
5	3	6.692735			6.728874	7.45883	7.085119	7.012676		
6	4	6.8831		Mean	6.77788	7.142292	6.771342	7.255937		
7	5	6.934702		StdDev	0.060754	0.280925	6.119746	7.678632		
8	6	7.167506					6.393192	7.069464		
31	29	7.161848					7.067572	7.325329		
32	30	7.188481					7.316917	6.744359		
33	31	7.052134				Mean	7.026196	7.051699		
34	32	7.559373				StdDev	0.479805	0.376885		
35	33	6.925036								
36	34	7.038894	% of diff mean		0.053765		0.00363	% of diff mean		
37			% of diff StdDev		3.623976		0.214504	% of diff StdDev		
38										

26. Highlight **E36:G37**. From the Tool bar, select the Percent Style icon.

27. From the Tool bar, select the Increase Decimal icon. Click one time.

This changes the format of the differences to percents with one place past the decimal.

	C	D	E	F	G	H	I	J	K
1			Sample	Sample	Sample	Sample			
2			of 3	of 3	of 30	of 30			
3			6.845856	7.04544	7.290466	6.476734			
4			6.758911	6.922607	6.952859	7.098922			
5			6.728874	7.45883	7.085119	7.012676			
6		Mean	6.77788	7.142292	6.771342	7.255937			
7		StdDev	0.060754	0.280925	6.119746	7.678632			
8					6.393192	7.069464			
31					7.067572	7.325329			
32					7.316917	6.744359			
33				Mean	7.026196	7.051699			
34				StdDev	0.479805	0.376885			
35									
36	% of diff mean		5.4%		0.4%	% of diff mean			
37	% of diff StdDev		362.4%		21.5%	% of diff StdDev			
38									

Each worksheet will be different. In the example above you can see that between the two samples of 3 each, the percent of difference in the means was 5.4% and the percent of difference in the standard deviation was 362.4%. Between the two samples of 30 each, the percent of difference in the means was only .4% and the percent of difference in the standard deviation was only 21.5%. There was more difference in the means and standard deviation of the smaller samples than of the larger samples. Also in the two samples of 30, the means, 7.03 and 7.05 are much closer to the population mean of the birth weights (7.04). Every sample will be different, but in general the larger samples should have less variation.

If you wish to show the results of this exercise, you can print only the first page of your worksheet by doing the following:

From the Menu bar, select File. Select Print. From the Print dialog box, select Page(s). In the From text box, key 1. In the To text box, key 1. Click OK.

If you wish, save your file as **rand-1**. Close your file.

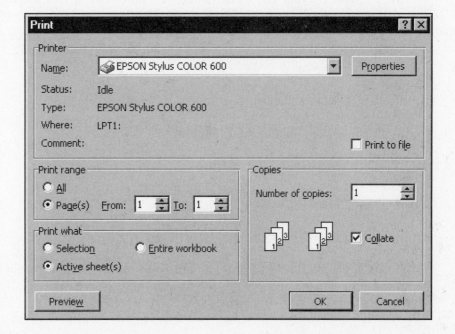

c. Plotting of Sample Means

Construct histograms using a very small sampling distribution of sample means and a larger sampling distribution of sample means.

1. On a new worksheet, enter the data as shown below.

	A	B	C	D	E	F	G	H	I	
1	Sample	Sample Values				Sample				
2	Number	1	2	3	Mean	Class	Freq			
3	1									
4	2									
5	3									
6	4									
7	5									
8	6									
9	7									
10	8									
11	9									
12	10									
13	11									
14	12									
15										

2. Make B3 your active cell. Key **=NORMINV(RAND(),7.04,.42)**. Press <Enter>.

3. Make B3 your active cell. Place your mouse arrow on the lower right handle of B3. Make sure you have a thick, black plus sign. Click your left mouse button twice, rapidly.

4. Highlight **B3:B14**. Place your mouse arrow on the lower right handle of B14. Drag B14 to C14:D14.

This generates random numbers.

5. In E3, key =**AVERAGE(B3:D3)**. Press <Enter>.

6. Using step 3, copy E3 to E4:E14.

This is the mean of each sample.

7. In F3 and F4, key **5.9** and **6.15**, respectively.

8. Highlight **F3:F4**. Place your mouse pointer on the lower right handle of F4. Drag to F5:F14.

This increases the weights in increments of .25 between 5.9 and 8.65.

9. Highlight **G3:G14**. With the range still highlighted, key =**FREQUENCY(E3:E14,F3:F14)** <u>DO NOT TOUCH THE <ENTER> KEY YET!</u>

10. After you have finished keying, hold down the <Shift> key and the <Ctrl> key together and at the same time touch the <Enter> key. The formula in the formula bar at the top of the worksheet should be inside curly brackets, { }.

This is called an *array*. An array links the data together and prevents the formula from being accidentally over-written.

Your worksheet should be similar to the one below. The numbers will be different but the format should be the same.

	A	B	C	D	E	F	G	H	I
1	Sample	Sample Values			Sample				
2	Number	1	2	3	Mean	Class	Freq		
3	1	7.002539	7.280273	7.187026	7.156613	5.9	0		
4	2	7.327805	6.956624	6.062287	6.782239	6.15	0		
5	3	6.172979	7.20566	7.690013	7.022884	6.4	0		
6	4	7.117397	7.202021	7.015982	7.1118	6.65	0		
7	5	7.360181	7.42049	6.095902	6.958858	6.9	2		
8	6	7.685653	6.674532	7.538569	7.299585	7.15	6		
9	7	6.769168	7.620385	6.497883	6.962478	7.4	3		
10	8	7.086487	7.031336	7.556749	7.224857	7.65	1		
11	9	7.742453	7.080808	7.38549	7.402917	7.9	0		
12	10	6.792978	7.117965	7.486402	7.132448	8.15	0		
13	11	7.325317	6.265432	6.596144	6.728964	8.4	0		
14	12	6.710974	6.930944	7.248558	6.963492	8.65	0		
15									

Touch the F9 function key on your keyboard. The numbers in the frequency column should change.

You will now plot the frequency distribution on a histogram.

11. Highlight **F3:G14**. From the Tool bar, select ChartWizard.

12. In Step 1, under Chart type, select Column. Under Chart sub-type, the upper left chart should be selected. Click Next.

13. In Step 2, at the top, select the Series tab. Under the Series list box, **Series1** should be highlighted. Select Remove. (We don't want the class as part of the values). At the bottom, in the Category (X) axis labels text box, click on the icon at the far right. Put your cursor on cell F3, click, hold and drag to cell F14. There will be a running box around cells **F3:F14**. Touch <Enter>. This identifies the class column as the x-axis labels. Click Next.

14. In Step 3, at the top, the Titles tab should be selected. Click on the Chart title text box, key **Mean Weights for Babies**. Tab to the Category (X) axis text box. Key **Interval Weights**. Tab to the Value (Y) axis text box. Key **Frequency**.

15. At the top, select the Legend tab. Click in the Show legend check box to de-select the legend. Click Finish.

16. Make sure the handles show on the chart box. With your **right** mouse arrow, click on one of the columns. Select Format Data Series.

17. At the top select the Options tab. In the Gap width text box, click on the down arrow until the Gap width reads 0. Click OK.

A condensed chart is displayed.

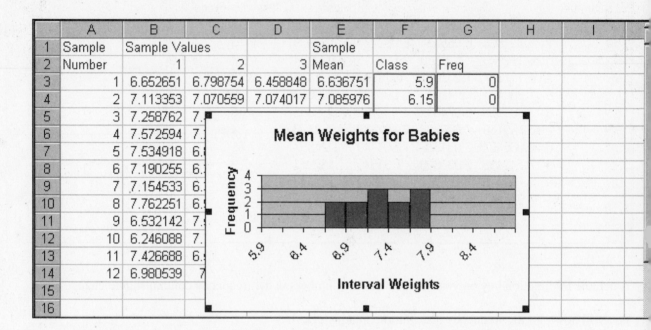

	A	B	C	D	E	F	G	H	I
1	Sample	Sample Values			Sample				
2	Number	1	2	3	Mean	Class	Freq		
3	1	6.652651	6.798754	6.458848	6.636751	5.9	0		
4	2	7.113353	7.070559	7.074017	7.085976	6.15	0		
5	3	7.258762	7.						
6	4	7.572594	7.						
7	5	7.534918	6.						
8	6	7.190255	6.						
9	7	7.154533	6.						
10	8	7.762251	6.						
11	9	6.532142	7.						
12	10	6.246088	7.						
13	11	7.426688	6.						
14	12	6.980539	7						
15									
16									

18. With the handles still on the chart, click and hold the left mouse button inside the chart. A 4-way arrow will show in the chart. As you move the chart it will show as an open box with dashed lines. With your mouse button still depressed, drag your mouse and move your chart so the left edge of the chart is in column H and the top edge of the chart is in row 2.

19. Click on your bottom scroll bar until you can see the columns for class and frequency and the chart all on the same screen.

20. Click on the bottom handle of the chart. Drag the bottom line to row 16.

Touch the F9 function key on your keyboard. The histogram will change according to the random weights selected.

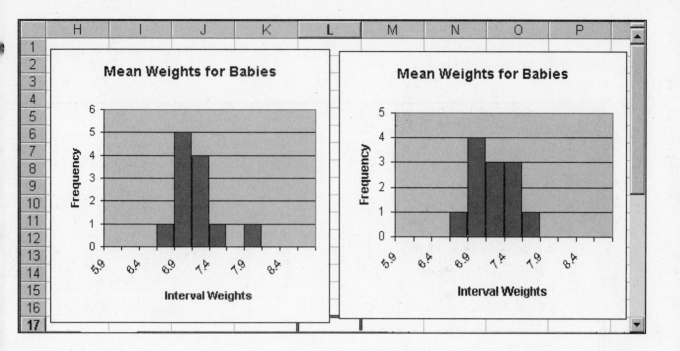

You will have a variety of charts that may resemble a normal curve, or they may appear skewed. Compare your chart with the two sample charts shown above. As you touch the F9 key your chart will change. At times it may look very different from the above example, or very similar.

If you wish to show the results of this exercise, you can print only the first page of your worksheet by doing the following. Highlight **A1:C1**. From the Menu bar, select Format. Select Column. Select Hide. This hides part of your worksheet so you can print more easily. From the Menu bar, select File. Select Print. From the Print dialog box, select Pages(s). In the From text box, key **1**. In the To text box, key **1**. Click OK.

To unhide the columns, from the Menu bar select Format. Select Column. Select Unhide.

You will now insert additional columns so you can observe how the frequency of the means changes when there is a larger sample.

21. Highlight **C1:AC1**. If you place your mouse arrow on the vertical scroll bar it will highlight the extra columns. From the Menu bar, select Insert. Select Columns.

This inserts extra columns between the existing columns so you will not have to re-enter the formulas for the mean and frequency.

22. Make B2 your active cell. From the Menu bar, select Edit. Select Fill. Select Series. From the Series dialog box, select Series in Rows. Select Type Linear. In the Step Value text box, key **1**. In the Stop Value text box, key **28**. Click OK.

23. In cell AD2:AE2, key **29** and **30**, respectively.

24. Highlight **B3:B14**. Drag the lower right handle of B14 to C14:AC14.

Click on the bottom scroll bar until your histogram is visible. Push the F9 function key several times. Notice how the histogram changes.

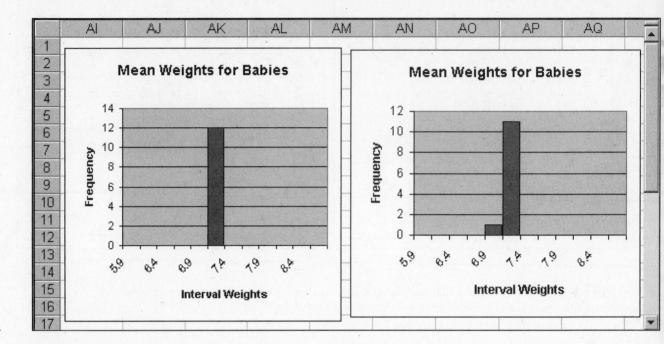

Compare your chart with the two sample charts shown above. Even though your chart changes, the bars are pretty much centered around the middle because taking the mean of several means reduces the amount of dispersion.

If you wish to show the results of this exercise, you can print only the first page of your worksheet by doing the following. Highlight **A1:AD1**. From the Menu bar, select F**o**rmat. Select **C**olumn. Select **H**ide. This hides part of your worksheet so you can print more easily. From the Menu bar, select File. Select Print. From the Print dialog box, select Pages(s). In the **F**rom text box, key **1**. In the **T**o text box, key **1**. Click OK.

If you wish save your worksheet as **rand-2**. Close your file.

Central Limits Theorem: Sampling From a Uniform Population

Example 2. A class of 32 statistics students were assigned to randomly select seven telephone numbers from a phone book. They were then asked to record the last digit of each phone number and find the mean of the seven numbers they recorded. This problem could illustrate the results of sampling from a uniform population if they created a histogram of the 32 sample means. It may look like the following example.

1. On a new worksheet, enter the data as shown.

	A	B	C	D	E	F	G	H	I	J	K	
1	Sample	Data							Sample			
2	Number	1	2	3	4	5	6	7	Mean	Interval	Freq	
3	1											
4												

2. Make A3 your active cell. From the Menu bar, select Edit. Select Fill. Select Series. From the Series dialog box, select Series in Columns. Select Type Linear. In the Step Value text box, key **1**. In the Stop Value text box, key **32**. Click OK.

3. Make B3 your active cell. Key =**RAND()*10**

4. Make B3 your active cell. Place your mouse arrow on the lower right handle of B3. Make sure you have a thick, black plus sign. Click your left mouse button twice, rapidly.

5. Highlight **B3:B34**. Place your mouse arrow on the lower right handle of B34. Drag B34 to C34:H34.

This generates random numbers.

6. While B3:H34 is still highlighted, from the Tool bar, select the Decrease Decimal icon several times   until all the figures appear as whole numbers.

7. Highlight **A1:H1**. From the Menu bar, select Format. Select Column. Select Width. In the Column Width text box, key 7. Click OK.

This decreases the width of your worksheet making it easier to view.

8. In I3 key =**AVERAGE(B3:H3)**

9. Make I3 your active cell. Place your mouse arrow on the lower right handle of I3. Make sure you have a thick, black plus sign. Click your left mouse button twice, rapidly.

10. In J3:J4, key **2.0** and **2.4**, respectively.

11. Highlight **J3:J4**. Place your mouse arrow on the lower right handle of J4, Drag to J5:J18.

12. Highlight **K3:K18**. With the range still highlighted, key =**FREQUENCY(I3:I34,J3:J18)**
    <u>DO NOT TOUCH THE <ENTER> KEY YET!</u>

13. After you have finished keying, hold down the <Shift> key and the <Ctrl> key together and at the same time touch the <Enter> key. The formula in the formula bar at the top of the worksheet should be inside curly brackets, { }.

Touch the F9 function key on your keyboard. The numbers in the frequency column should change.

You will now plot the frequency distribution on a histogram.

14. Highlight **J3:K18**. From the Tool bar, select ChartWizard.

15. In Step 1, under Chart type, select Column. Under Chart sub-type, the upper left chart should be selected. Click Next.

16. In Step 2, at the top, select the Series tab. Under the Series list box, **Series1** should be highlighted. Select Remove. (We don't want the Interval as part of the values). At the bottom, in the Category (X) axis labels text box, click on the icon at the far right. Put your cursor on cell J3, click, hold and drag to cell J18. There will be a running box around cells **J3:J18**. Touch <Enter>. This identifies the Interval column as the x-axis labels. Click Next.

17. In Step 3, at the top, the Titles tab should be selected. Click on the Chart title text box, key **Uniform Sample**. Tab to the Category (X) axis text box. Key **Sample Means**. Tab to the Value (Y) axis text box. Key **Frequency**.

18. At the top, select the Legend tab. Click in the Show legend check box to de-select the legend. Click Finish.

19. Make sure the handles show on the chart box. With your **right** mouse arrow, click on one of the columns. Select Format Data Series.

20. At the top, select the Options tab. In the Gap width text box, click on the down arrow until the Gap width reads 0. Click OK.

A condensed chart is displayed.

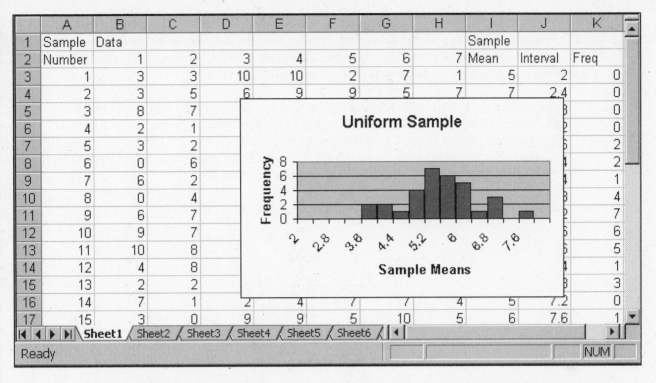

	A	B	C	D	E	F	G	H	I	J	K
1	Sample	Data							Sample		
2	Number	1	2	3	4	5	6	7	Mean	Interval	Freq
3	1	3	3	10	10	2	7	1	5	2	0
4	2	3	5	6	9	9	5	7	7	2.4	0
5	3	8	7								0
6	4	2	1								0
7	5	3	2								2
8	6	0	6								2
9	7	6	2								1
10	8	0	4								4
11	9	6	7								7
12	10	9	7								6
13	11	10	8								5
14	12	4	8								1
15	13	2	2								3
16	14	7	1	2	4	7	7	4	5	7.2	0
17	15	3	0	9	9	5	10	5	6	7.6	1

Sheet1 / Sheet2 / Sheet3 / Sheet4 / Sheet5 / Sheet6 /

Ready   NUM

21. With the handles still on the chart, click and hold the left mouse button inside the chart. A 4-way arrow will show in the chart. As you move the chart it will show as an open box with dashed lines. With your mouse button still depressed, drag your mouse and move your chart so the left edge of the chart is in column L and the top edge of the chart is in row 3.

22. Click on your bottom scroll bar until you can see the columns for Interval and Frequency and the chart all on the same screen.

23. Click on the bottom handle of the chart. Drag the bottom line to row 17.

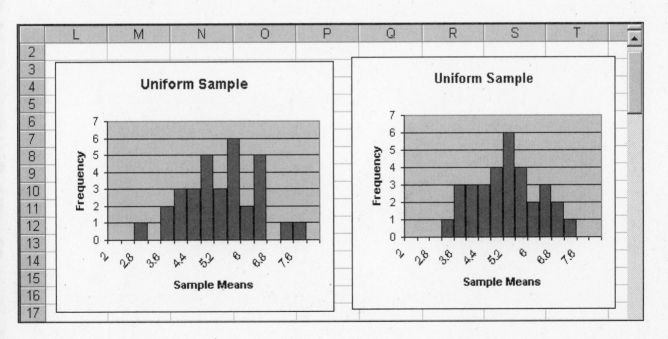

Touch the F9 function key on your keyboard and compare with the two sample charts shown above. The histogram will change according to the sample means selected. You will have a variety of charts but they should approximate a normal curve because of the central limits theorem.

If you wish to show the results of this exercise, you can print only the first page of your worksheet by doing the following. Highlight **A1:G1**. From the Menu bar, select Format. Select Column. Select Hide. This hides part of your worksheet so you can print more easily. From the Menu bar, select File. Select Print. From the Print dialog box, select Pages(s). In the From text box, key **1**. In the To text box, key **1**. Click OK.

If your wish, save your file as **rand-3**. Close your file.

Practice Exercises taken from textbook.

8-1. The following table lists the most recent data available on per capita personal income (in dollars) for each of 50 states. (Textbook problem 8-41)

No.	New England		No.	Plains		No.	Southwest	
1	Connecticut	39,300	17	Iowa	25,615	36	Arizona	25,189
2	Maine	24,603	18	Kansas	26,824	37	New Mexico	21,853
3	Massachusetts	35,551	19	Minnesota	30,793	38	Oklahoma	22,953
4	New Hampshire	31,114	20	Missouri	26,376	39	Texas	26,858
5	Rhode Island	29,377	21	Nebraska	27,049		**Rocky Mountain**	
6	Vermont	25,889	22	North Dakota	23,313	40	Colorado	31,546
	Mideast		23	South Dakota	25,045	41	Idaho	22,835
7	Delaware	30,778		**Southeast**		42	Montana	22,019
8	Maryland	32,465	24	Alabama	22,987	43	Utah	23,288
9	New Jersey	35,551	25	Arkansas	22,244	44	Wyoming	26,396
10	New York	33,890	26	Florida	27,780		**Far West**	
11	Pennsylvania	28,605	27	Georgia	27,340	45	Alaska	28,577
	Great Lakes		28	Kentucky	23,237	46	California	29,910
12	Illinois	31,145	29	Louisiana	22,847	47	Hawaii	27,544
13	Indiana	26,143	30	Mississippi	20,688	48	Nevada	31,022
14	Michigan	28,113	31	North Carolina	26,003	49	Oregon	27,023
15	Ohio	27,152	32	South Carolina	23,545	50	Washington	30,392
16	Wisconsin	27,390	33	Tennessee	25,574			
			34	Virginia	29,789			
			35	West Virginia	20,888			

a. Generate a random frequency distribution of per capita personal income.
b. From the frequency distribution, select two small samples (sample size of 4) and two large samples (sample size of 40), and compare the means and standard deviations.
c. Construct histograms using a very small sampling distribution of sample means (sample size of 3) and a larger sampling distribution of sample means (sample size of 30). As you touch the F9 key to give you different charts, what do you notice between the charts of small sampling distributions and of larger sampling distributions?

8-2 Using the same data on per capita personal income found in problem 8-1, illustrate the central limit theorem. Use a sample size of 8 and create a histogram of the sample means.

CHAPTER
9
ESTIMATION AND CONFIDENCE INTERVALS

CHAPTER GOALS

After completing this chapter, you will be able to:

1. Define a point estimate.

2. Define level of confidence.

3. Use Excel to calculate a confidence interval for a population mean when the sample size is 30 or larger.

4. Use Excel to calculate a confidence interval for a proportion when the sample size is 30 or larger.

5. Use Excel to determine the sample size for estimating the population mean.

6. Use Excel to determine the sample size for estimating the population proportion.

Introduction

The previous chapter introduced **sampling** and the **central limit theorem**. We stressed that it is usually not feasible to inspect the entire population. Excel was used to show that the means of small samples have more dispersion or scatter than the means of large samples. We also used Excel to illustrate the **central limit theorem**. That is if all samples of a particular size are selected from any population, the sampling distribution of the sample mean is approximately a normal distribution. This approximation improves with larger samples.

In most situations we use sampling to find a **point estimate**, one number used to describe the population. Often only one number is not very useful if we do not know the dispersion or scatter. This chapter uses Excel to find a more informative estimate that presents a range of values in which the population value is expected to occur or a **confidence interval** of the population.

Point estimates are sample measures of central tendency such as mean, median and mode. Sample measures of dispersion such as variance and standard deviation are also point estimates.

Confidence intervals state the range within which a population parameter probably lies. The specified probability is called the *level of confidence*. A 95 percent confidence interval means that we have a 95 percent level of confidence that a similarly constructed interval will contain the parameter being estimated.

Chapter 9

Frequently we need to determine the size of a sample. How many people should we contact to find the popularity of a political candidate or an idea? How many items do we examine to ensure product quality? This chapter uses Excel to calculate confidence intervals for population means and population proportions, and to determine sample size for estimating a mean or a proportion.

Confidence Intervals for a Population Mean

Example 1. The wildlife department has been feeding a special food to rainbow trout fingerlings in a pond. A sample of the weights of 40 trout revealed that the mean weight is 402.7 grams and the standard deviation 8.8 grams. What are the 99 percent confidence limits?

The 99 percent confidence interval is $\overline{X} \pm z \dfrac{s}{\sqrt{n}}$, where

$\overline{X}$ is the point estimate of the population mean.

The *z-value* depends on the level of confidence required.
   A 99 percent confidence results in a z-value of 2.58.
   A 95 percent confidence results in a z-value of 1.96.
   A 90 percent confidence results in a z-value of 1.645.

s is the sample standard deviation.

n is the number of samples.

1. On a new worksheet enter the data as shown below.

	A	B	C	D	E	F	G	H	I
1	Confidence Interval-Mean								
2									
3	Mean=								
4	z=								
5	StdDev=								
6	n=								
7	Confidence Limits								
8	Lower	Upper							
9									

2. In A9, type **=B3-B4*B5/SQRT(B6)**

3. In B9, type **=B3+B4*B5/SQRT(B6)**

110

The cell contents for A9 and B9 display #DIV/0!. This is because you have not yet entered the variables.

	A	B	C	D	E	F	G	H	I
1	Confidence Interval-Mean								
2									
3	Mean=								
4	z=								
5	StdDev=								
6	n=								
7	Confidence Limits								
8	Lower	Upper							
9	#DIV/0!	#DIV/0!							
10									

    4. Save your file as **cnfdinv**.

All you need to do now is enter the variable numbers.

    5. In B3:B6, enter respectively, **402.7**, **2.58**, **8.8**, and **40**

	A	B	C	D	E	F	G	H	I
1	Confidence Interval-Mean								
2									
3	Mean=	402.7							
4	z=	2.58							
5	StdDev=	8.8							
6	n=	40							
7	Confidence Limits								
8	Lower	Upper							
9	399.1102	406.2898							
10									

The lower and upper limits are displayed.

Confidence Interval for a Population Proportion

Example 2. A market survey was conducted to estimate the proportion of homemakers who could recognize the brand name of a cleanser based on the shape and color of the container. Of the 1,400 homemakers surveyed, 420 were able to identify the brand name. What are the 99 percent confidence limits?

The 99 percent confidence interval is $p \pm z\sqrt{\dfrac{p(1-p)}{n}}$, where:

p is the sample proportion.

The *z-value* depends on the level of confidence required, as in example 3.

n is the sample size.

    1. On the same worksheet enter the data as shown in E1:F7.

	A	B	C	D	E	F	G	H	I
1	Confidence Interval-Mean				Confidence Interval-Proportion				
2									
3	Mean=	402.7			Propor=				
4	z=	2.58			z=				
5	StdDev=	8.8			n=				
6	n=	40			Confidence Limits				
7	Confidence Limits				Lower	Upper			
8	Lower	Upper							
9	399.1102	406.2898							
10									

    2. In E8, key =**F3-F4*SQRT(F3*(1-F3)/F5)**

    3. In F8, key =**F3+F4*SQRT(F3*(1-F3)/F5)**

The cell contents for E8 and F8 display #DIV/0!. This is because you have not yet entered the variables.

	A	B	C	D	E	F	G	H	I
1	Confidence Interval-Mean				Confidence Interval-Proportion				
2									
3	Mean=	402.7			Propor=				
4	z=	2.58			z=				
5	StdDev=	8.8			n=				
6	n=	40			Confidence Limits				
7	Confidence Limits				Lower	Upper			
8	Lower	Upper			#DIV/0!	#DIV/0!			
9	399.1102	406.2898							
10									

All you need to do now is enter the variable numbers.

4. In F3, key =**420/1400**

This is the proportion of the sample.

5. In F4, key **2.58**

The confidence level is 99 percent.

6. In F5, key **1400**

The lower and upper limits are displayed.

	A	B	C	D	E	F	G	H	I
1	Confidence Interval-Mean				Confidence Interval-Proportion				
2									
3	Mean=	402.7			Propor=	0.3			
4	z=	2.58			z=	2.58			
5	StdDev=	8.8			n=	1400			
6	n=	40			Confidence Limits				
7	Confidence Limits				Lower	Upper			
8	Lower	Upper			0.268402	0.331598			
9	399.1102	406.2898							
10									

If you wish, save your worksheet as **cnfdinv1**. Close your file.

Example 3. Determining a sample size for means.

The formula for determining a sample size for a mean is $n=\left[\dfrac{z\cdot s}{E}\right]^2$

The *z-value* depends on the level of confidence required.
A 99 percent confidence results in a z-value of 2.58.
A 95 percent confidence results in a z-value of 1.96.
A 90 percent confidence results in a z-value of 1.645.

s is the estimate of the population standard deviation.

E is the maximum allowable error.

Problem: A student in Public Administration wants to conduct a study to determine the mean amount members of city councils earn. The error in estimating the mean is to be less than $100 with a 95 percent level of confidence. The student found a report by the Department of Labor that estimated the standard deviation to be $1,000. What is the sample size?

1. On a new worksheet, in A1, key **Sample size for mean**.

2. In A3, key **z-value=**

3. in A4, key **StdDev=**

4. In A5, key **error=**

5. In A6 key **sample size=**

6. In A7, key **rounded=**

7. Place your mouse arrow between the columns of A and B. Double click your left mouse button. Column A widens to accommodate the text.

8. In B6, key **=((B3*B4)/B5)^2**

The contents of B6 will display #DIV/0!. It will change when you fill in the values.

	A	B	C	D	E	F	G	H	I
1	Sample size for mean								
2									
3	Z-value=								
4	StdDev=								
5	error=								
6	sample size=	#DIV/0!							
7	rounded=								
8									

9. In B3, key **1.96**, since the confidence required is 95 percent.

10. In B4, key **1000**, the estimated standard deviation.

11. In B5, key **100**, since the error is to be less than 100.

The sample size of 384.16 is displayed in B6.

12. In B7, key **=INT(B6+.99)** This rounds up the answer to the next whole number of 385.

13. Bold the contents of A1 and B7.

	A	B	C	D	E	F	G	H	I
1	Sample size for mean								
2									
3	Z-value=	1.96							
4	StdDev=	1000							
5	error=	100							
6	sample size=	384.16							
7	rounded=	**385**							
8									

Example 4. Determining a sample size for proportion.

The formula for determining a sample size for a proportion is $n = p(1-p)\left(\dfrac{z}{E}\right)^2$

The *z-value* depends on the level of confidence required, as in example 5.

p is the population proportion if known. If the proportion is not known, p is assigned a value of .5.

E is the margin of error in the proportion that is requested.

Problem: The student in Public Administration also wants to estimate the proportion of cities that have private refuse collectors. The student wants the estimate to be within .10 of the population proportion, the desired level of confidence is 90 percent, and no estimate is available for the population proportion. What is the required sample size?

1. On the same worksheet as example 3, in cell A9, key **Sample size for proportion.**

2. In A11, key **z-value=**

3. In A12, key **PopPro=**

4. In A13, key **error=**

5. In A14, key **sample size=**

6. In B14, key **=B12*(1-B12)*(B11/B13)^2**

7. In B15, key **rounded=**

The contents of B14 will display #DIV/0!. It will change when you fill in the values.

8. In B11, key **1.645**, since the confidence required is 90 percent.

9. In B12, key **.5**, since the population proportion is not known.

10. In B13, key **.10**, since the error should not exceed 10 percent.

The sample size of 67.65063 is displayed in B14.

11. In B15 key, **=INT(B14+.99)** This rounds up the answer to the next whole number of 68.

12. Bold the contents of A9 and B15.

	A	B	C	D	E	F	G	H	I
1	**Sample size for mean**								
2									
3	Z-value=	1.96							
4	StdDev=	1000							
5	error=	100							
6	sample size=	384.16							
7	rounded=	**385.00**							
8									
9	**Sample size for proportion**								
10									
11	Z-value=	1.645							
12	PopPro=	0.5							
13	error=	0.1							
14	sample size=	67.65063							
15	rounded=	**68.00**							
16									

If you wish, save your worksheet as **sampsize**.

You can do more than one problem on a worksheet. Just copy the formulas on another part of the worksheet. For example if you wanted to find another sample size for proportion, you would highlight A9:B15. From the Tool bar, you could click your mouse arrow on the copy button. You would make the cell active where you wanted the formula to be, for instance, E1, then you would click your mouse arrow on the paste button, and touch the <Enter> key. Be sure to identify each problem and bold the answer to identify it more easily.

Practice Exercises taken from textbook.

9-1. A random sample of 85 group leaders, supervisors, and similar personnel at General Motors revealed that, on the average, a person spent 6.5 years on the job before being promoted. The standard deviation of the sample was 1.7 years. Using the .95 degree of confidence, construct the confidence interval within which the population mean lies. (Textbook Problem 9-31)

9-2. There are 20,000 eligible voters in York County of South Carolina. A random sample of 500 York County voters revealed 350 plan to vote to return Louella Miller to the state senate. Construct a 99 percent confidence interval for the proportion of voters in the county who plan to vote for Ms. Miller. From this sample information can you confirm she will be re-elected? (Textbook Problem 9-47)

9-3. We want to estimate the population mean within 5, with a 99 percent level of confidence. The population standard deviation is estimated to be 15. How large a sample is required? (Textbook Problem 9-24)

9-4. The estimate of the population proportion is to be within + or - .10, with a 99 percent level of confidence. The best estimate of the population proportion is .45. How large a sample is required? (Textbook Problem 9-26)

CHAPTER
10
ONE-SAMPLE TESTS OF HYPOTHESIS

CHAPTER GOALS

After completing this chapter, you will be able to:

1. Define a hypothesis and hypothesis testing.

2. Use Excel to conduct a z-test of hypothesis about a population mean when the sample size is greater than 30 or with a known population standard deviation.

3. Use Excel to conduct a t-test of hypothesis for a small sample involving a population mean.

4. Use Excel to conduct a z-test of hypothesis about a population proportion.

Introduction

Chapter 8 and 9 dealt with a segment of statistical inference called estimation. This chapter will deal with a method of testing those estimations. Hypothesis testing is a procedure based on sample evidence and probability theory. It is used to determine whether the hypothesis is a reasonable statement and should not be rejected, or is unreasonable and should be rejected.

The terms, **hypothesis testing** and **testing a hypothesis** are used interchangeably. Hypothesis testing starts with a statement, or assumption about a population parameter. We then analyze the differences between the results actually observed and the results we would expect to obtain if some underlying hypothesis were actually true. When we do this we also evaluate the risks involved in making these decisions based on sample information and the interrelationship of these risks based on sample size. In this chapter and several of the following chapters, numerous hypothesis testing procedures will be presented that are frequently employed in the analysis of data obtained from studies and experiments designed under a variety of conditions. The following statements could be tested using hypothesis techniques:

⬜ A college dean says the mean age of students is 25.

⬜ A medical center study shows a new procedure is more than 82 percent successful.

⬜ Q Lube claims the average waiting time for their customers is less than 17 minutes.

Steps in hypothesis testing:

These five steps in hypothesis testing will help you solve a wide variety of hypothesis problems, not just those using a z test for large samples. The five step process provides a similar format and a thread of continuity that can be helpful in recognizing different statistical tests and knowing which test to apply different situations.

1. **State the null and alternative hypothesis** using either formulas or words.
   The Null Hypothesis (H_o) is the statement of "no change" or significant difference.

   The Alternative Hypothesis (H_1) is the statement that there is a significant difference. When direction is stated it is a one-directional test (one-tailed). When direction is not stated it is a two-directional test (two-tailed).

2. **Select the level of significance** or the probability that the null hypothesis is rejected when, in fact, it is true.

3. **Select the test statistic** you will be using: the z test, t test, f test, Chi Square test, etc.

4. **Formulate the decision rule**. Using a picture or curve that estimates the distribution you are testing, show the critical value if you are performing a one-directional test or the upper and lower critical values if you are performing a two-directional test.

5. **Make a Decision**. State the results of the hypothesis test in terms of the question using complete sentences and examples.

In Chapter 10 you will be using formulas to solve problems. You will also need to build an Excel worksheet before completing a hypothesis test. In building this worksheet, it is often helpful to use names in a formula instead of cell references. The following exercise will give you some experience naming cells and using the names in a formula:

$$\mu = \frac{\Sigma X}{N}$$

Remember, to switch to formula view, hold the control key down while tapping the tilde key. You may have to adjust the column width to be able to view the entire formula.

Example 1. There are 6 students in a computer class. Their test scores were 92, 96, 61, 86, 79, and 84. What is the mean test grade?

The formula for finding the population mean is sum of all the values in the population divided by the number of values in the population.

1. On a new worksheet, enter the following as shown.

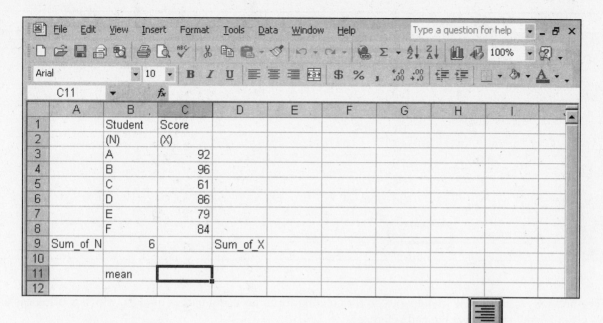

2. Highlight **B3:B8**. From the Tool bar, click on the Align Right button.

3. Highlight **C3:C8**. From the Tool bar, click on the AutoSum button.

The sum of X (498) is displayed in cell C9.

4. Highlight **A9:B9**. From the Menu bar, select Insert. Select Name. Select Create. Select the check box for Left Column. Click OK.

Notice that when B9 is selected as the active cell, the name of the cell (Sum_of_N) shows in the Name box in the upper left corner.

5. Highlight **C9:D9**. From the Menu bar, select Insert. Select Name. Select Create. Select the check box for Right Column. Click on OK.

Notice that when C9 is selected as the active cell, the name of the cell (Sum_of_X) shows in the Name box in the upper left corner.

6. Make C11 your active cell. Key =**Sum_of_X/Sum_of_N**. Touch <Enter>. The population mean (83) is displayed.

You could have keyed the formula =C9/B9, but you used the names of those cells instead.

Notice that when C11 is selected as the active cell, the formula =Sum_of_X/Sum_of_N shows in the Formula bar at the top of the worksheet.

	A	B	C	D	E	F	G	H	I
	C11	▼	= =Sum_of_X/Sum_of_N						
1		Student	Score						
2		(N)	(X)						
3		A	92						
4		B	96						
5		C	61						
6		D	86						
7		E	79						
8		F	84						
9	Sum_of_N	6	498	Sum_of_X					
10									
11		mean	83						
12									

The previous exercise was to prepare you for creating formulas using names of cells, which is often easier to visualize than using just the cell references.

You will create a worksheet for hypothesis testing of large samples. It can be used for one left-tail, one right-tail, or a two-tailed hypothesis test. After the worksheet is created, you will be able to enter the input data. The worksheet will compute the results for all three kinds of hypothesis tests. You must then decide which one is needed for your test.

A Test of Hypothesis About One Sample Mean From a Population with a known population standard deviation or a sample greater than 30.

The worksheet you create will include formulas used in your textbook. The symbols will often be referred to as names. The formula for finding the test statistic z is $z = \dfrac{\overline{X} - \mu}{\sigma / \sqrt{n}}$.

$\overline{X}$ is the sample mean. It will be referred to as SaMean.

μ is the hypothesis mean. It will be referred to as HoMean.

σ is the population standard deviation or it is the standard deviation of the sample which is used to estimate the population standard deviation. It will be referred to as StdDev.

n is the sample number. It will be referred to as n.

Example 2 Creating a worksheet for testing of normal hypothesis of a one sample (population) mean.

   1. On a new worksheet, enter the following data as shown.

	A	B	C	D	E	F	G	H	I
1	Test of Normal Hypotheses:								
2	One Sample Mean								
3									
4	Input Data								
5	HoMean								
6	SaMean								
7	n								
8	StdDev								
9	Alpha								
10	Calculated Value								
11	z								
12	Test for Left-Tail								
13	LftCrt_zVal								
14	Conclusion								
15	p-value								
16	Test for Right-Tail								
17	RtCrt_zVal								
18	Conclusion								
19	p-value								
20	Test for Two-Tail								
21	AbsCrt_zVal								
22	Conclusion								
23	p-value								
24									

   2. Widen column A by double clicking your mouse arrow between column headings A and B.

   3. Highlight **A5:A9**. From the Tool bar, click on the Align Right button.

   4. Right Align cell A11. Right align Cells A13:A15. Right align Cells A17:A19.
      Right align cells A21:A23.

	A	B	C	D	E	F	G	H
1	Test of Normal Hypotheses:							
2	One Sample Mean							
3								
4	Input Data							
5	HoMean							
6	SaMean							
7	n							
8	StdDev							
9	Alpha							
10	Calculated Value							
11	z							
12	Test for Left-Tail							
13	LftCrt_zVal							
14	Conclusion							
15	p-value							
16	Test for Right-Tail							
17	RtCrt_zVal							
18	Conclusion							
19	p-value							
20	Test for Two-Tail							
21	AbsCrt_zVal							
22	Conclusion							
23	p-value							

5. Highlight **A5:B9**. From the Menu bar, select Insert. Select Name. Select Create. Select the check box for Left Column. Click on OK. The cells B5:B9 have names as well as cell references.

6. Highlight **A11:B11**. Use the same method from step 5 to create a name.

7. Use step 5 to create a name for A13:B13, A17:B17, and A21:B21

8. Make B11 your active cell. Key =**(SaMean-HoMean)/(StdDev/SQRT(n))** Touch <Enter>.

This is the formula for finding z.

The output result in cell B11 shows #DIV/0! This is because none of the input data have values yet (so the formula is trying to divide by 0). When you start entering the input data, the formulas will generate the correct output.

9. Make B13 your active cell. Key =**NORMSINV(Alpha)** Touch <Enter>.

This is the formula for finding the left critical value of z. There is no value for the output because there has been no input data.

As you key the remaining formulas, there will be no output value for any of the cells. The values will be obtained when the input data is entered later.

After each formula is completed, touch the <Enter> key. If you make a mistake and have already entered the formula, double click your mouse arrow on the cell and you will be able to edit the cell without rekeying the entire contents.

10. Make B17 your active cell. Key =**-NORMSINV(Alpha)**

This is the formula for finding the right critical value of z.

11. Make B21 your active cell. Key =**ABS(NORMSINV(Alpha/2))**

This is the formula for finding the critical value of z on a two-tailed test.

12. Make B14 your active cell. Key =**If(z<LftCrt_zVal, "Reject Ho","Do Not Reject Ho")**

This is the decision to reject or not to reject the null hypothesis of a left-tail test. If the test statistic of z is less than the left critical z value, then the hypothesis is rejected. Otherwise do not reject the null hypothesis.

13. Make B18 your active cell. Key =**If (z>RtCrt_zVal, "Reject Ho", "Do Not Reject Ho")**

This is the decision to reject or not to reject the null hypothesis of a right-tail test. If the test statistic of z is greater than the right critical z value, then the hypothesis is rejected. Otherwise do not reject the null hypothesis.

14. Make B22 your active cell. Key =**If (OR(z<-AbsCrt_zVal, z>AbsCrt_zVal), "Reject Ho", "Do Not Reject Ho")**

This is a decision to reject or not to reject the null hypothesis of a two-tailed test. If the test statistic of z is less than the negative critical z value *or* if the test statistic of z is greater than the critical z value, then reject the hypothesis. Otherwise do not reject the hypothesis.

You now need to enter the formula for the p-value for each of the three tests.

15. Make B15 your active cell. Key =**NORMSDIST(z)**

16. Make B19 your active cell. Key =**1-NORMSDIST(z)**

17. Make B23 your active cell. Key =**If(z>0,2*(1-NORMSDIST(z)),2*NORMSDIST(z))**

As you are entering the formulas, your worksheet will display the cell contents as shown below.

	A	B	C	D	E	F	G	H
1	Test of Normal Hypotheses:							
2	One Sample Mean							
3								
4	Input Data							
5	HoMean							
6	SaMean							
7	n							
8	StdDev							
9	Alpha							
10	Calculated Value							
11	z	=(SaMean-HoMean)/(StdDev/SQRT(n))						
12	Test for Left-Tail							
13	LftCrt_zVal	=NORMSINV(Alpha)						
14	Conclusion	=IF(z<LftCrt_zVal, "Reject Ho", "Do Not Reject Ho")						
15	p-value	=NORMSDIST(z)						
16	Test for Right-Tail							
17	RtCrt_zVal	=-NORMSINV(Alpha)						
18	Conclusion	=IF(z>RtCrt_zVal, "Reject Ho","Do Not Reject Ho")						
19	p-value	=1-NORMSDIST(z)						
20	Test for Two-Tail							
21	AbsCrt_zVal	=ABS(NORMSINV(Alpha/2))						
22	Conclusion	=IF(OR(z<-AbsCrt_zVal,z>AbsCrt_zVal),"Reject Ho","Do Not Reject Ho")						
23	p-value	=IF(z>0,2*(1-NORMSDIST(z)),2*NORMSDIST(z))						
24								

After you have finished entering all the formulas, your worksheet will appear as shown below.

	A	B	C	D	E	F	G	H
1	Test of Normal Hypotheses:							
2	One Sample Mean							
3								
4	Input Data							
5	HoMean							
6	SaMean							
7	n							
8	StdDev							
9	Alpha							
10	Calculated Value							
11	z	#DIV/0!						
12	Test for Left-Tail							
13	LftCrt_zVal	#NUM!						
14	Conclusion	#DIV/0!						
15	p-value	#DIV/0!						
16	Test for Right-Tail							
17	RtCrt_zVal	#NUM!						
18	Conclusion	#DIV/0!						
19	p-value	#DIV/0!						
20	Test for Two-Tail							
21	AbsCrt_zVal	#NUM!						
22	Conclusion	#DIV/0!						
23	p-value	#DIV/0!						
24								

Save a copy of this worksheet so you can enter data into the input cells and not have to recreate the worksheet each time. Save as **1sa-mean.**

Example 3. The mean annual turnover rate of the 200 count bottle of Bayer Aspirin was reported to be 6.0. (This indicates that the stock of Bayer turns over on the pharmacy shelves an average of 6 times per year.) The standard deviation is 0.50. It is suspected that the actual mean turnover has changed and is not 6.0. The .05 significance level is to used to test this hypothesis. A random sample of 64 bottles of the 200 count size Bayer Aspirin showed a mean of 5.84. Shall we reject the hypothesis that the population mean is 6.0?

    1. Open the file **1sa-mean** if it is not already active.

    2. In cells B5:B9, enter the input data in the appropriate cells, as shown below.

	A	B	C	D	E	F	G	H
1	Test of Normal Hypotheses:							
2	One Sample Mean							
3								
4	Input Data							
5	HoMean	6						
6	SaMean	5.84						
7	n	64						
8	StdDev	0.5						
9	Alpha	0.05						
10								

The values in the output cells have automatically changed to reflect the input data.

	A	B	C	D	E	F	G	H
1	Test of Normal Hypotheses:							
2	One Sample Mean							
3								
4	Input Data							
5	HoMean	6						
6	SaMean	5.84						
7	n	64						
8	StdDev	0.5						
9	Alpha	0.05						
10	Calculated Value							
11	z	-2.56						
12	Test for Left-Tail							
13	LftCrt_zVal	-1.64485						
14	Conclusion	Reject Ho						
15	p-value	0.005234						
16	Test for Right-Tail							
17	RtCrt_zVal	1.644853						
18	Conclusion	Do Not Reject Ho						
19	p-value	0.994766						
20	Test for Two-Tail							
21	AbsCrt_zVal	1.959961						
22	Conclusion	Reject Ho						
23	p-value	0.010467						
24								

You can then interpret the results. Since the calculated value for z of -2.56 is lower than -1.959961, we reject the null hypotheses. The rejection area is the area outside $\pm$ the absolute value of z.

The mean turnover rate of the 200 count bottle of Bayer Aspirin is not 6.0. The p-value tells you that you have a .010467 chance of rejecting a true null hypothesis (a type one error).

If you wish, save your worksheet as **example3**. Close your file.

A Test of Hypothesis About a Population Mean: Small Sample, Population Standard Deviation Unknown

If the sample size is small or less than 30 observations and the standard deviation is unknown, the z distribution is not appropriate. In this case, the **student t**, or the **t distribution**, is used as the test statistic.

The formula for a population t test is: $t = \dfrac{\overline{X} - \mu}{s/\sqrt{n}}$

$\overline{X}$ is the mean of the small sample. It will be referred to as SaMean.

μ is the hypothesized population mean. It will be referred to as HoMean.

s is the standard deviation of the sample. It will be referred to as StdDev.

n is the sample size. It will be referred to as n.

The decision to reject or not to reject the hypothesis (the t test) is very similar to the decision using the z test.

You will rename some cells, edit the formulas of some cells, and re-key the formulas in other cells. The formula for t tests requires the use of the degrees of freedom, df.

df is found by the formula df = n-1.

Example 4. Creating a worksheet for testing a population mean for a small sample.

1. Open **1sa-mean**.

2. Make A11 your active cell. From the Menu bar, select Insert. Select Row.

The variables in A5:A9 remain the same as for large samples, however some are computed differently.

3. Make B6 your active cell. Key =**AVERAGE(Sample)**. (Don't forget to touch the <Enter> key after entering each cell's contents.)

This computes the mean of your sample data, which you will enter later.

4. Make B8 your active cell. Key =**STDEV(Sample)**

This computes the standard deviation of your sample data, which you will enter later.

5. In cell A11, key **df**

6. Right align A11.

7. Highlight **A11:B11** From the Menu bar, select Insert. Select Name. Select Create. Select Left Column. Click OK.

8. Make B11 your active cell. Key **=n-1**

This computes the degrees of freedom.

9. In A12, key **t**

10. Highlight **A12:B12**. Repeat the instructions in step 7 for creating a name.

You will notice that when B12 is your active cell, the name of the cell (t) shows in the name box in the upper left corner. B12 used to have the name z. You have renamed the cell, *t*.

11. Make A14 your active cell. Double click the left mouse button.

A gray shadow box appears around the cell. The cell can now be edited.

12. Use the left arrow key to move the flashing vertical bar to the left of the letter z. Touch the <delete> key once. Key the letter **t**. (Remember to touch the <Enter> key when you are finished with editing).

Cell A14 should now read, LftCrt_tVal.

13. Make B14 your active cell. Key **=-TINV(2*Alpha,df)**

This replaces the old formula for LftCrt_zVal with the new formula for LftCrt_tVal.

14. Highlight **A14:B14**. Use the instructions in step 7 for creating a name.

15. Make B15 your active cell. Double click the left mouse button to edit the cell. Using your arrow keys to move the flashing vertical bar, delete the letter z both times and replace with the letter **t**.

Cell B15 should now read, =IF(t<LftCrt_tVal, "Reject Ho", "Do Not Reject Ho")

16. Make B16 your active cell. Key **=If(t<0,TDIST(ABS(t),df,1),1-TDIST(t,df,1))**

This replaces the old formula for *p* with the new formula using the t test.

You will continue to edit some cell contents and rekey others.

17. Make A18 your active cell. Double click to edit the cell. Replace the letter z with the letter **t**.

Cell A18 should now read RtCrt_tVal.

18. Make B18 your active cell. Key **=TINV(2*Alpha,df)**

19. Highlight **A18:B18**. Use the instructions in step 7 for creating a name.

20. Make B19 your active cell. Double click to edit the cell. Delete the letter z both times and replace with the letter **t**.

Cell B19 should now read, =If(t>RtCrt_tVal, "Reject Ho", "Do Not Reject Ho")

21. Make B20 your active cell. Key **=IF(t>0, TDIST(t,df,1),1-TDIST(ABS(t),df,1))**

22. Make A22 your active cell. Double click to edit the cell. Replace the letter z with the letter **t**.

Cell A 22 should now read, AbsCrt_tVal.

23. Make B22 your active cell. Key **=TINV(Alpha, df)**

24. Highlight **A22:B22**. Use the instructions in step 7 for creating a name.

25. Make B23 your active cell. Double click to edit the cell. Delete the letter z each time and replace with the letter **t**.

Cell B23 should now read, = IF(OR(t<-AbsCrt_tVal,t>AbsCrt_tVal), "Reject Ho", "Do not Reject Ho")

26. Make B24 your active cell. Key **=TDIST(ABS(t),df,2)**

After you have finished editing, and re-keying the worksheet, it should have the cell contents as shown below.

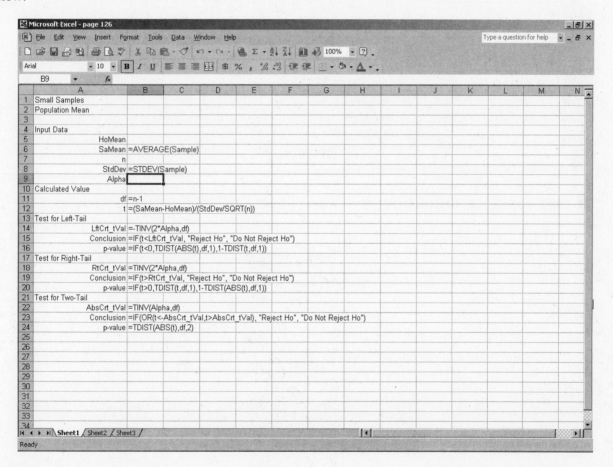

The worksheet should appear as shown below.

	A	B	C	D	E	F	G	H
1	Small Samples							
2	Population Mean							
3								
4	Input Data							
5	HoMean							
6	SaMean	#NAME?						
7	n							
8	StdDev	#NAME?						
9	Alpha							
10	Calculated Value							
11	df	-1						
12	t	#NAME?						
13	Test for Left-Tail							
14	LftCrt_tVal	#NUM!						
15	Conclusion	#NAME?						
16	p-value	#NAME?						
17	Test for Right-Tail							
18	RtCrt_tVal	#NUM!						
19	Conclusion	#NAME?						
20	p-value	#NAME?						
21	Test for Two-Tail							
22	AbsCrt_tVal	#NUM!						
23	Conclusion	#NAME?						
24	p-value	#NAME?						
25								

Save this worksheet as **t-tst1mn**.

Example 5. A machine is set to fill a small bottle with 9.0 grams of medicine. It is claimed that the mean weight is less than 9.0 grams. The hypothesis is to be tested at the .01 level. A sample revealed these weights (in grams): 9.2, 8.7, 8.9, 8.6, 8.8, 8.5, 8.7, and 9.0. Is the claim valid?

1. Open the file **t-tst1mn**, if it is not already open.

2. Make D1 your active cell. Key **Sample**.

Don't forget to touch the <Enter> key after entering the contents of each cell.

3. In D2:D9, key in the sample weights as shown below.

	A	B	C	D	E	F	G	H
1	Small Samples			Sample				
2	Population Mean			9.2				
3				8.7				
4	Input Data			8.9				
5	HoMean			8.6				
6	SaMean	#NAME?		8.8				
7	n			8.5				
8	StdDev	#NAME?		8.7				
9	Alpha			9				
10								

4. Highlight **D1:D9**. From the Menu bar, select Insert. Select Name. Select Create. Select Top Row. Click OK.

This gives the sample weights a name (Sample), so you can use them in the formulas you created for SaMean and StdDev.

5. Enter the remaining data in cells B5, B7, and B9 as shown below.

	A	B	C	D	E	F	G	H
1	Small Samples			Sample				
2	Population Mean			9.2				
3				8.7				
4	Input Data			8.9				
5	HoMean	9		8.6				
6	SaMean	8.8		8.8				
7	n	8		8.5				
8	StdDev	0.226779		8.7				
9	Alpha	0.01		9				
10	Calculated Value							
11	df	7						
12								

After you are through entering the formulas and data, the values in the output cells have automatically changed to reflect the input data.

	A	B	C	D	E	F	G	H
1	Small Samples			Sample				
2	Population Mean			9.2				
3				8.7				
4	Input Data			8.9				
5	HoMean	9		8.6				
6	SaMean	8.8		8.8				
7	n	8		8.5				
8	StdDev	0.226779		8.7				
9	Alpha	0.01		9				
10	Calculated Value							
11	df	7						
12	t	-2.49444						
13	Test for Left-Tail							
14	LftCrt_tVal	-2.99795						
15	Conclusion	Do Not Reject Ho						
16	p-value	0.020664						
17	Test for Right-Tail							
18	RtCrt_tVal	2.997949						
19	Conclusion	Do Not Reject Ho						
20	p-value	0.979336						
21	Test for Two-Tail							
22	AbsCrt_tVal	3.499481						
23	Conclusion	Do Not Reject Ho						
24	p-value	0.041327						
25								

You can now interpret the results. Accept the H_0. At the .01 significance the mean weight of the small bottles of medicine is not significantly different from 9.0 grams.

If you wish, save your file as **ex5t-tst**. Close your file.

A Test of Hypothesis About a Single Proportion

In the last exercise you created a worksheet used to conduct a test of hypothesis about small sample population means. You will again make some changes to a previously created worksheet. This worksheet will then be used to test a hypothesis about a single proportion.

The formula for finding z is

$$z = \frac{p - \pi}{\sqrt{\frac{\pi(1-\pi)}{n}}}$$

p   is the proportion in the sample possessing the trait. It will be referred to as *p*.

π   is the hypothesized population proportion. It will be referred to as *pi*.

n   is the size of the sample. It will be referred to as *n*.

Example 6. Creating a worksheet for testing of hypothesis about a single proportion.

1. Retrieve the file **1sa-mean**.

2. Make A2 your active cell. Key **Single Proportion.**

3. Highlight **A5:A8**. From the Menu bar, select Edit. Select Delete. Select Entire Row. Click OK.

This will delete the contents of the rows and the names of the cells that were created.

4. Highlight **A5:A7**. From the Menu bar, select Insert. Select Rows.

This will give you blank rows to insert your input data.

5. In A5:A7, key the input variables, as shown below.

	A	B	C	D	E	F	G	H
1	Test of Normal Hypotheses:							
2	Single Proportion							
3								
4	Input Data							
5	p							
6	pi							
7	n							
8	Alpha							
9	Calculated Value							
10	z	#REF!						
11								

6. Highlight **A5:A7**. From the Tool bar, select Align Right.

Chapter 10

7. Highlight **A5:B7**. From the Menu bar, select <u>I</u>nsert. Select <u>N</u>ame. Select <u>C</u>reate. Select <u>L</u>eft Column. Click OK. Select <u>Y</u>es, for Replace Existing definition of "n"?

Excel remembers *n* was used in an earlier worksheet. You are redefining *n*.

8. Make B10 your active cell. You will key the new formula for z. As you key, the previous formula for z will be replaced. Key **=(p-pi)/SQRT(pi*(1-pi)/n)**

z	▼	= =(p-pi)/SQRT(pi*(1-pi)/n)						
	A	B	C	D	E	F	G	H
1	Test of Normal Hypotheses:							
2	Single Proportion							
3								
4	Input Data							
5	p							
6	pi							
7	n							
8	Alpha							
9	Calculated Value							
10	z	#DIV/0!						
11	Test for Left-Tail							
12	LftCrt_zVal	#NUM!						
13	Conclusion	#DIV/0!						
14	p-value	#DIV/0!						
15								

Save the worksheet as **1-propor**.

Example 7. This claim is to be investigated at the .01 level: "Forty percent or more of those persons who retired from an industrial job before the age of 60 would return to work if a suitable job were available." Seventy-four persons out of the 200 sampled said they would return to work.
Is the claim valid?

1. Open the file **1-propor** if it is not already active.

2. In cell B5, key **=74/200**

By keying in the equation =74/200, you are computing the sample proportion.

3. In B6:B8, enter the input data in the appropriate cells as shown below.

	A	B	C	D	E	F	G	H
1	Test of Normal Hypotheses:							
2	Single Proportion							
3								
4	Input Data							
5	p	0.37						
6	pi	0.4						
7	n	200						
8	Alpha	0.01						
9								

The values in the output cells have automatically changed to reflect the input data.

	A	B	C	D	E	F	G	H
1	Test of Normal Hypotheses:							
2	Single Proportion							
3								
4	Input Data							
5	p	0.37						
6	pi	0.4						
7	n	200						
8	Alpha	0.01						
9	Calculated Value							
10	z	-0.86603						
11	Test for Left-Tail							
12	LftCrt_zVal	-2.32634						
13	Conclusion	Do Not Reject Ho						
14	p-value	0.193238						
15	Test for Right-Tail							
16	RtCrt_zVal	2.326342						
17	Conclusion	Do Not Reject Ho						
18	p-value	0.806762						
19	Test for Two-Tail							
20	AbsCrt_zVal	2.575835						
21	Conclusion	Do Not Reject Ho						
22	p-value	0.386476						
23								

You can now interpret the results. Since the calculated value for z of -0.86603 is greater than -2.32634, we accept the null hypothesis. The question was "forty percent or more" so this is a one tailed test.

Forty percent or more of those persons who retired from an industrial job before the age of 60 would return to work if a suitable job were available. The p-value shows that you have a .193238 chance of rejecting a true null hypothesis (a type one error) which is much higher than .01.

If you wish, save your worksheet as **example7**. Close your file.

Practice Exercises taken from textbook.

In addition to showing your printout, state the results of the hypothesis test in terms of the question using complete sentences and examples.

10-1. The MacBurger restaurant chain claims that the mean waiting time of customers for service is normally distributed with a mean of 3 minutes and a standard deviation of 1 minute. The quality-assurance department found in a sample of 50 customers at the Warren Road MacBurger that the mean waiting time was 2.75 minutes. At the .05 significance level, can we say that the mean waiting time is less than 3 minutes? (Textbook Problem 10-6)

10-2. A new weight-watching company, Weight Reducers International, advertises that those who join will lose, on the average, 10 pounds the first two weeks. A random sample of 50 people who joined the new weight reduction program revealed the mean loss to be 9 pounds. The standard deviation of the sample was computed to be 2.8 pounds. At the .05 level of significance, can we conclude that those joining Weight Reducers on average will lose less than 10 pounds? Determine the p-value.
(Textbook Problem 10-29)

10-3. According to a recent survey Americans get a mean of seven hours sleep per night. A random sample of 50 students at West Virginia University revealed the mean number of hours slept last night was 6 hours and 48 minutes (6.8 hours). The standard deviation of the sample was 0.9 hours. Is it reasonable to conclude that the students at West Virginia sleep less than the typical American? (Textbook Problem 10-31)

10-4. According to the Coffee Research Organization (http://www.coffeeresearch.org) the typical American coffee drinker consumes an average of 3.1 cups per day. A sample of 12 senior citizens reveled they consumed the following amounts, reported in cups, of coffee yesterday. (Textbook Problem 10-45)

| 3.1 | 3.3 | 3.5 | 2.6 | 2.6 | 4.3 | 4.4 | 3.8 | 3.1 | 4.1 | 3.1 | 3.2 |

At the .05 significance level, does this sample data suggest there is a difference between the national average and the sample information from senior citizens?

10-5. NBC news, in a segment on the price of gasoline, reported last evening that the mean price nationwide is $1.50 per gallon, for self-serve regular unleaded. A random sample of 35 stations in the Milwaukee, WI, area revealed that the mean price was $1.52 per gallon and that the standard deviation was $0.05 per gallon. At the .05 significance level can we conclude that the price of gasoline is higher in the Milwaukee area? (Textbook Problem 10-35)

10-6. The Myers Summer Casual Furniture Store tells customers that a special order will take six weeks (42) days. During recent months the owner has received several complaints that the special orders are taking longer than 42 days. A sample of 12 special orders delivered in the last month showed than the mean waiting time was 51 days with a standard deviation of 8 days. At the .05 significance level, are customers waiting an average of more than 42 days? Textbook Problem (10-43)

10-7. The National Safety Council reported in Vitality that 52 percent of American turnpike drivers are men. A sample of 300 cars traveling eastbound on the New Jersey Turnpike yesterday revealed that 170 were driven by men. At the .01 significance level, can we conclude that a larger proportion of men were driving on the New Jersey Turnpike than the national statistics indicate? (Textbook Problem 10-11)

10-8. The policy of the Suburban Transit Authority is to add a bus route if more than 55 percent of the potential commuters indicate they would use the particular route. A sample of 70 commuters revealed that 42 would use a proposed route from Bowman Park to the downtown area. Does the Bowman-to-downtown route meet the STA criteria? Use the .05 significance level. (Textbook Problem 10-38)

10-9. From past experience a television manufacturer found that 10 percent or less of its sets needed any type of repair in the first two years of operation. In a sample of 50 sets manufactured 2 years ago, 9 needed repair. At the .05 significance level, has the percent of sets needing repair increased? Determine the p-value. (Textbook Problem 10-40)

CHAPTER
11
TWO-SAMPLE TESTS OF HYPOTHESIS

CHAPTER GOALS

After completing this chapter, you will be able to:

1. Use Excel to conduct a z test of a hypothesis about the difference between two independent population means, both samples 30 or more.

2. Use Excel to conduct a t test of a hypothesis involving the difference between two population means, when at least one sample is less than 30.

3. Use Excel to conduct a test of hypothesis about the difference between two population proportions.

4. Use Excel to conduct a t test of a hypothesis about the mean difference between paired or dependent observations.

Introduction

Chapter 10 dealt with tests of hypothesis using one sample. This chapter will deal with **hypothesis testing of two samples.** As stated in chapter 10, hypothesis testing is a procedure based on sample evidence and probability theory. It is used to determine whether the hypothesis is a reasonable statement and should not be rejected, or is unreasonable and should be rejected.

Steps in hypothesis testing for Two Samples remain the same:

1. **State the null and alternative hypothesis** using either formulas or words. The Null Hypothesis (H_o) is the statement of "no change" or significant difference.

   The Alternative Hypothesis (H_1) is the statement that there is a significant difference. When direction is stated it is a one-directional test (one-tailed). When direction is not stated it is a two-directional test (two-tailed).

2. **Select the level of significance** or the probability that the null hypothesis is rejected when, in fact, it is true.

3. **Select a test statistic** you will be using: the z test, t test, F test, Chi Square test, etc.

4. **Formulate a decision rule**. Using a picture or curve that estimates the distribution you are testing, show the critical value if you are performing a one-directional test or the upper and lower critical values if you are performing a two-directional test.

5. **Make a decision**. State the results of the hypothesis test in terms of the question using complete sentences and examples.

A Test of Hypothesis Between Sample Means From Two Independent Populations with both Samples 30 or More

In the last chapter you created a worksheet used to conduct a test of hypothesis about a sample mean from a single population. You will make some changes to that worksheet to use in other situations. The next will be a test of hypothesis between sample means from two populations. The value of z, the critical value, is computed differently.

$$z = \frac{\overline{X_1} - \overline{X_2}}{\sqrt{\dfrac{s_1^2}{n_1} + \dfrac{s_2^2}{n_2}}}$$

$\overline{X_1}$ is the mean of the first sample. It will be referred to as X1_mean.

$\overline{X_2}$ is the mean of the second sample. It will be referred to as X2_mean.

s_1 is the standard deviation of the first sample. It will be referred to as s1_StdDev.

s_2 is the standard deviation of the second sample. It will be referred to as s2_StdDev.

n_1 is the first sample number. It will be referred to as n1_sample.

n_2 is the second sample number. It will be referred to as n2_sample.

Example 1. Creating a worksheet for testing of hypothesis between two population means.

1. Retrieve the file **1sa-mean**.

2. Make A2 your active cell. Key **Two Sample Means**.

3. Highlight **A5:A8**. From the Menu bar, select <u>E</u>dit. Select <u>D</u>elete. Select Entire <u>R</u>ow. Click OK.

This will delete the contents of the rows and the names of the cells that were created.

4. Highlight **A5:A10**. From the Menu bar, select <u>I</u>nsert. Select <u>R</u>ows.

This will give you blank rows to insert your input data.

5. In A5:A10, key the input variables, as shown on the next page.

	A	B	C	D	E	F	G	H
1	Test of Normal Hypotheses:							
2	Two Sample Means							
3								
4	Input Data							
5	X1_mean							
6	X2_mean							
7	s1_StdDev							
8	s2_StdDev							
9	n1_sample							
10	n2_sample							
11								

6. Highlight **A5:A10**. From the Tool bar, select Align Right.

7. Highlight **A5:B10**. From the Menu bar, select Insert. Select Name. Select Create. Select Left Column. Click on OK.

8. Make B13 your active cell. You will key a new formula for z. As you key, the formula created for z used with one sample mean will be replaced by the new formula. You will use the shift key with the number 6 to key the ^ symbol.
   Key **=(X1_mean-X2_mean)/SQRT((s1_StdDev^2/n1_sample)+(s2_StdDev^2/n2_sample))**

z	▼	=	=(X1_mean-X2_mean)/SQRT((s1_StdDev^2/n1_sample)+(s2_StdDev^2/ n2_sample))

	A	B						
1	Test of Normal Hypotheses:							
2	Two Sample Means							
3								
4	Input Data							
5	X1_mean							
6	X2_mean							
7	s1_StdDev							
8	s2_StdDev							
9	n1_sample							
10	n2_sample							
11	Alpha							
12	Calculated Value							
13	z	#DIV/0!						
14								

Save the worksheet as filename **2sa-mean**.

Example 2. Corngrow is a chemical specifically designed to add weight to corn during the growing season. Alternate acres were treated with Corngrow during the growing season. In order to determine whether or not Corngrow was effective, 400 ears of corn receiving the Corngrow treatment were selected at random. Each was weighed, and the mean weight was computed to be 16 ounces, with a standard deviation of 1 ounce. Likewise, 100 ears of untreated corn were weighed. The mean was 15.7 ounces, and the standard deviation was 1.2 ounces. Using a one-tailed test and the .05 level, can we say that Corngrow was effective in adding weight to the corn?

    1. Open the file **2sa-mean** if it is not already active.

    2. In B5:B11, enter the input data in the appropriate cells as shown below.

	A	B	C	D	E	F	G	H
1	Test of Normal Hypotheses:							
2	Two Sample Means							
3								
4	Input Data							
5	X1_mean	16						
6	X2_mean	15.7						
7	s1_StdDev	1						
8	s2_StdDev	1.2						
9	n1_sample	400						
10	n2_sample	100						
11	Alpha	0.05						
12								

The values in the output cells have automatically changed to reflect the input data.

	A	B	C	D	E	F	G	H
1	Test of Normal Hypotheses:							
2	Two Sample Means							
3								
4	Input Data							
5	X1_mean	16						
6	X2_mean	15.7						
7	s1_StdDev	1						
8	s2_StdDev	1.2						
9	n1_sample	400						
10	n2_sample	100						
11	Alpha	0.05						
12	Calculated Value							
13	z	2.307692						
14	Test for Left-Tail							
15	LftCrt_zVal	-1.64485						
16	Conclusion	Do Not Reject Ho						
17	p-value	0.989492						
18	Test for Right-Tail							
19	RtCrt_zVal	1.644853						
20	Conclusion	Reject Ho						
21	p-value	0.010508						
22	Test for Two-Tail							
23	AbsCrt_zVal	1.959961						
24	Conclusion	Reject Ho						
25	p-value	0.021016						
26								

You can now interpret the results. Since the calculated value for z of 2.307692 is greater than 1.64485, we reject the null hypothesis. This is a one tailed test, and the rejection area is the area greater than 1.644853 (RtCrt_zVal), since we are only interested in finding if Corngrow adds weight to the corn.

Corngrow was effective in adding weight to the corn. The p-value shows that you have a .010508 chance of rejecting a true null hypothesis (a type one error.)

If you wish, save your worksheet as **example2**. Close your file.

Two Population Means when at Least One Sample is Less Than 30

Excel has a pre-prepared dialog box to use for t-tests with two sample means. You will do the following problem using the Data Analysis dialog box:

Example 3. The production supervisor at Corry Steel Company, a manufacturer of steel desks, wants to compare the number of defective desks produced on the day shift versus the number produced on the afternoon shift. A sample of the production from 6 day shifts and 8 afternoon shifts revealed the following information:

Day	5	8	7	6	9	7		
Afternoon	8	10	7	11	9	12	14	9

At the .05 significance level, is there a difference in the mean number of defects per shift?

    1. In cells A1:B9, enter the data for Edne and Orno as shown below.

	A	B	C	D	E	F	G	H	I
1	Day	Afternoon							
2	5	8							
3	8	10							
4	7	7							
5	6	11							
6	9	9							
7	7	12							
8		14							
9		9							
10									

From the Menu Bar, select Tools. If Data Analysis does not appear, select Add-Ins. Select Analysis ToolPak. Click OK.

    2. From the Menu bar, select Tools. Select Data Analysis. Place your mouse arrow on the down arrow of the side scroll bar. Select t-Test: Two Sample Assuming Equal Variances. Click OK.

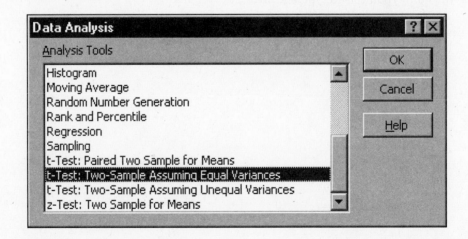

The dialog box for t-Test: Two Sample Assuming Equal Variances is displayed.

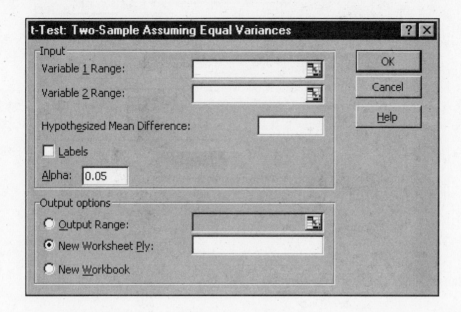

3. Your cursor should be on the Variable 1 Range text box: Key **A1:A7**. Touch the tab key.

4. In the Variable 2 Range: text box, key **B1:B9**. Touch the tab key.

5. In the Hypothesized Mean Difference text box, key **0**. Touch the tab key.

6. Select the Labels check box. Touch the tab key.

7. In the Alpha text box, key **.05** if it is not already displayed.

8. Select the Output Range check box. In the text box, key **E1**. Click OK.

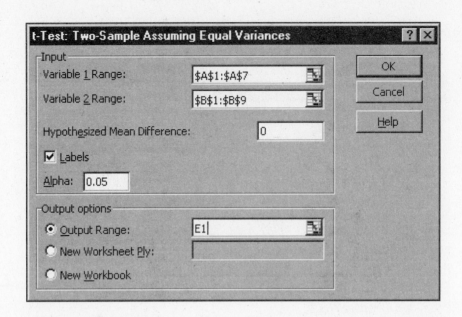

The output data is displayed, but is hard to read.

	A	B	C	D	E	F	G	H	I
1	Day	Afternoon			t-Test: Two-Sample Assuming Equal Variances				
2	5	8							
3	8	10				*Day*	*Afternoon*		
4	7	7			Mean	7	10		
5	6	11			Variance	2	5.142857		
6	9	9			Observatio	6	8		
7	7	12			Pooled Va	3.833333			
8		14			Hypothesi:	0			
9		9			df	12			
10					t Stat	-2.8372			
11					P(T<=t) on	0.007487			
12					t Critical o	1.782287			
13					P(T<=t) tw	0.014974			
14					t Critical tv	2.178813			
15									

Make E8 your active cell. From the Menu bar, select Format. Select Column. Select AutoFit Selection.

	A	B	C	D	E	F	G
1	Day	Afternoon			t-Test: Two-Sample Assuming Equal Variances		
2	5	8					
3	8	10				Day	Afternoon
4	7	7			Mean	7	10
5	6	11			Variance	2	5.142857
6	9	9			Observations	6	8
7	7	12			Pooled Variance	3.833333	
8		14			Hypothesized Mean Difference	0	
9		9			df	12	
10					t Stat	-2.8372	
11					P(T<=t) one-tail	0.007487	
12					t Critical one-tail	1.782287	
13					P(T<=t) two-tail	0.014974	
14					t Critical two-tail	2.178813	
15							

The output is now easier to read and can be interpreted.

Reject the H_o and accept the H_1. The computed t statistic (-2.8372) is less than the negative critical value for a two tailed t test (-2.178813).* There is a difference in the mean number of defects between the afternoon shift and the day shift at the .05 level of significance. (* H_o is rejected if the t Stat is greater than the t Critical two-tail or less than a negative value of the t Critical two-tail.)

Save as **ex3t-tst**.

A Test of Hypothesis About Two Population Proportions

The last large samples hypothesis with which you will be working is to conduct a test about two population proportions. You will make changes to a previously created worksheet one more time. The formula for finding z changes also.

$$z = \frac{p_1 - p_2}{\sqrt{\dfrac{p_c(1-p_c)}{n_1} + \dfrac{p_c(1-p_c)}{n_2}}}$$

p_1 is the ratio of the first sample. It will be referred to as p1_ratio.

p_1 is found by the formula $p_1 = \dfrac{X_1}{n_1}$

X_1 is the number in the first sample that possess the trait. It will be referred to as X1_sample.

n_1 is the total number in the first sample. It will be referred to as n1_total.

p_2 is the ratio of the second sample. It will be referred to as p2_ratio.

p_2 is found by the formula $p_2 = \dfrac{X_2}{n_2}$

X_2 is the number in the second sample that possess the trait. It will be referred to as X2_sample.

n_2 is the total number in the second sample. It will be referred to as n2_total.

p_c is the pooled estimate of the population proportion. It will be referred to as pc_est.

p_c is found by the formula $p_c = \dfrac{(X_1 + X_2)}{(n_1 + n_2)}$

Example 4. Creating a worksheet for testing of hypothesis about two population proportions.

1. Retrieve the file **1sa-mean**.

2. Make A2 your active cell. Key **Two Population Proportions**.

3. Highlight **A5:A8**. From the Menu bar, select Edit. Select Delete. Select Entire Row. Click OK.

This will delete the contents of the rows and the names of the cells that were created.

4. Highlight **A5:A11**. From the Menu bar, select Insert. Select Rows.

This will give you blank rows to insert your input data.

5. In A5:A11, key the input variable names as shown below.

	A	B	C	D	E	F	G	H
1	Test of Normal Hypotheses:							
2	Two Population Proportions							
3								
4	Input Data							
5	p1_ratio							
6	p2_ratio							
7	X1_sample							
8	X2_sample							
9	n1_total							
10	n2_total							
11	pc_est							
12	Alpha							
13	Calculated Value							
14								

6. Right Align A5:A11.

7. Create names for A5:B11.

8. Make B5 your active cell. Key =**X1_sample/n1_total**

9. Make B6 your active cell. Key **=X2_sample/n2_total**

10. Make B11 your active cell. Key = **(X1_sample+X2_sample)/(n1_total+n2_total)**

11. Make B14 your active cell. As you key, the previous formula for z will be replaced. Key =**(p1_ratio-p2_ratio)/SQRT((pc_est*(1-pc_est)/n1_total)+(pc_est*(1-pc_est)/n2_total))**

| z | ▼ | = | =(p1_ratio-p2_ratio)/SQRT((pc_est*(1-pc_est)/n1_total)+(pc_est*(1-pc_est)/ n2_total)) |

	A	
1	Test of Normal Hypotheses:	
2	Two Population Proportions	
3		
4	Input Data	
5	p1_ratio	#DIV/0!
6	p2_ratio	#DIV/0!
7	X1_sample	
8	X2_sample	
9	n1_total	
10	n2_total	
11	pc_est	#DIV/0!
12	Alpha	
13	Calculated Value	
14	z	#DIV/0!
15		

Save the worksheet as **2-propor**.

Example 5. Of 150 adults who tried a new peach flavored peppermint patty, 87 rated it excellent. Of 200 children sampled, 123 rated it excellent. Using the .10 level of significance, can we conclude that there is a significant difference in the proportion of adults versus children who rate the new flavor as excellent?

1. Open the file **2-propor** if it is not already active.

2. In B7:B10 and B12, enter the input data in the appropriate cells as shown below.

	A	B	C	D	E	F	G	H
1	Test of Normal Hypotheses:							
2	Two Population Proportions							
3								
4	Input Data							
5	p1_ratio	#DIV/0!						
6	p2_ratio	#DIV/0!						
7	X1_sample	87						
8	X2_sample	123						
9	n1_total	150						
10	n2_total	200						
11	pc_est	#DIV/0!						
12	Alpha	0.1						
13	Calculated Value							
14	z	#VALUE!						
15								

The values in the output cells have automatically changed to reflect the input data.

	A	B	C	D	E	F	G	H
1	Test of Normal Hypotheses:							
2	Two Population Proportions							
3								
4	Input Data							
5	p1_ratio	0.58						
6	p2_ratio	0.615						
7	X1_sample	87						
8	X2_sample	123						
9	n1_total	150						
10	n2_total	200						
11	pc_est	0.6						
12	Alpha	0.1						
13	Calculated Value							
14	z	-0.66144						
15	Test for Left-Tail							
16	LftCrt_zVal	-1.28155						
17	Conclusion	Do Not Reject Ho						
18	p-value	0.254166						
19	Test for Right-Tail							
20	RtCrt_zVal	1.281551						
21	Conclusion	Do Not Reject Ho						
22	p-value	0.745834						
23	Test for Two-Tail							
24	AbsCrt_zVal	1.644853						
25	Conclusion	Do Not Reject Ho						
26	p-value	0.508331						
27								

You can now interpret the results. This is a two-tailed test because there was no direction stated. Accept the null hypothesis. There is not a significant difference in the proportion of adults versus children who rate the candy excellent.

If you wish, save your worksheet as **example5**. Close your file.

Paired or Dependent Observations

Excel also has a dialog box to use with paired observations. You will do the following problem using the Data Analysis dialog box.

Example 6. Advertisements by Sylph Fitness Center claim that completion of their course will result in the loss of weight. A random sample of 8 recent students showed the following body weights before entering the course and after the completion of the course. At the .01 significance level can we conclude that the students lost weight?

Name	Before	After
Hunter	155	154
Cashman	228	207
Mervine	141	147
Massa	162	157
Creola	211	196
Peterson	164	150
Redding	164	150
Poust	172	165

1. Open the file **ex3t-tst**. On this same worksheet, beginning with row 16, enter the data in columns A, B, and C as shown below.

	A	B	C	D	E	F	G
1	Day	Afternoon			t-Test: Two-Sample Assuming Equal Variances		
2	5	8					
3	8	10				Day	Afternoon
4	7	7			Mean	7	10
5	6	11			Variance	2	5.142857
6	9	9			Observations	6	8
7	7	12			Pooled Variance	3.833333	
8		14			Hypothesized Mean Difference	0	
9		9			df	12	
10					t Stat	-2.8372	
11					P(T<=t) one-tail	0.007487	
12					t Critical one-tail	1.782287	
13					P(T<=t) two-tail	0.014974	
14					t Critical two-tail	2.178813	
15							
16	Name	Before	After				
17	Hunter	155	154				
18	Cashman	228	207				
19	Mervine	141	147				
20	Massa	162	157				
21	Creola	211	196				
22	Peterson	164	150				
23	Redding	164	150				
24	Poust	172	165				
25							

From the Menu Bar, select Tools. If Data Analysis does not appear, select Add-Ins. Select Analysis ToolPak. Click OK.

2. From the Menu bar, select Tools. Select Data Analysis. Place your mouse arrow on the down arrow of the side scroll bar. Select t-Test: Paired Two Samples for Means. Click OK.

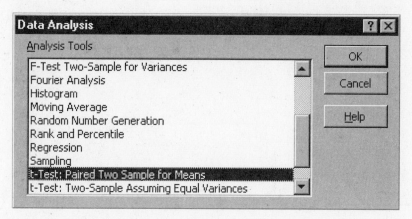

The dialog box for t-Test: Paired Two Sample for Means, is displayed.

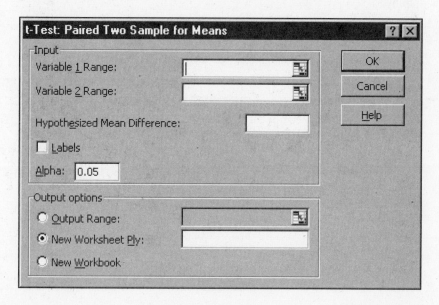

3. Your cursor should be in the Variable 1 Range text box. Key **B16:B24**. Touch the tab key.

4. In the Variable 2 Range text box, key **C16:C24**. Touch the tab key.

5. In the Hypothesized Mean Difference text box, key **0**. Touch the tab key.

6. Select the Labels check box. Touch the tab key.

7. In the Alpha text box, key **.01** if it is not already displayed.

8. Select the Output Range check box. In the text box, key **E16**. Click OK.

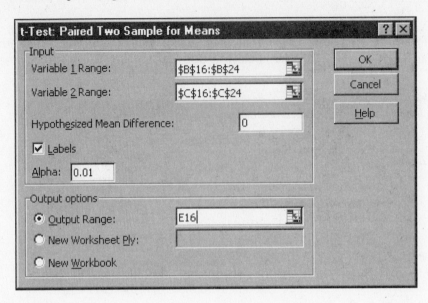

The output data is displayed.

	A	B	C	D	E	F	G
16	Name	Before	After		t-Test: Paired Two Sample for Means		
17	Hunter	155	154				
18	Cashman	228	207			Before	After
19	Mervine	141	147		Mean	174.625	165.75
20	Massa	162	157		Variance	868.5536	525.6429
21	Creola	211	196		Observations	8	8
22	Peterson	164	150		Pearson Correlation	0.974726	
23	Redding	164	150		Hypothesized Mean Difference	0	
24	Poust	172	165		df	7	
25					t Stat	2.861003	
26					P(T<=t) one-tail	0.012151	
27					t Critical one-tail	2.997949	
28					P(T<=t) two-tail	0.024303	
29					t Critical two-tail	3.499481	
30							

Accept the H_o. The computed t statistic (2.861003) is less than the t Critical one-tail (2.997949). We cannot conclude that the students lost weight at the .01 level of significance.

You can use worksheets for more than one problem. Since these are both t-tests we put them on the same worksheet. Make sure you use the same column for the output so the labels are in the same expanded column.

If you wish, you may print both exercises 3 and 6.

	A	B	C	D	E	F	G
1	Day	Afternoon			t-Test: Two-Sample Assuming Equal Variances		
2	5	8					
3	8	10				Day	Afternoon
4	7	7			Mean	7	10
5	6	11			Variance	2	5.142857
6	9	9			Observations	6	8
7	7	12			Pooled Variance	3.833333	
8		14			Hypothesized Mean Difference	0	
9		9			df	12	
10					t Stat	-2.8372	
11					P(T<=t) one-tail	0.007487	
12					t Critical one-tail	1.782287	
13					P(T<=t) two-tail	0.014974	
14					t Critical two-tail	2.178813	
15							
16	Name	Before	After		t-Test: Paired Two Sample for Means		
17	Hunter	155	154				
18	Cashman	228	207			Before	After
19	Mervine	141	147		Mean	174.625	165.75
20	Massa	162	157		Variance	868.5536	525.6429
21	Creola	211	196		Observations	8	8
22	Peterson	164	150		Pearson Correlation	0.974726	
23	Redding	164	150		Hypothesized Mean Difference	0	
24	Poust	172	165		df	7	
25					t Stat	2.861003	
26					P(T<=t) one-tail	0.012151	
27					t Critical one-tail	2.997949	
28					P(T<=t) two-tail	0.024303	
29					t Critical two-tail	3.499481	
30							

If you wish, save as **ex3&6t-tst**. Close your file.

Chapter 11

Practice Exercises taken from textbook.

In addition to showing your printout, state the results of the hypothesis test in terms of the question using complete sentences and examples.

11-1.   A nationwide sample of influential Republicans and Democrats were asked as a part of a comprehensive survey whether they favored lowering the environmental standards so that high-sulfur coal could be burned in coal-fired power plants. The results were: (Textbook Problem 11-11)

	Republicans	Democrats
Number sampled	1,000	800
Number in favor	200	168

At the .02 level of significance, can we conclude that there is a larger proportion of Democrats in favor of lowering the standards?

11-2. Fry Brothers heating and Air Conditioning, Inc. employs Larry Clark and George Murnen to make service calls to repair furnaces and air conditioning units in homes. Tom Fry, the owner, would like to know whether there is a difference in the mean number of service calls they make per day. A random sample of 40 days last year showed that Larry Clark made an average of 4.77 calls per day, with a standard deviation of 1.05 calls per day. For a sample of 50 days George Murnen made an average of 5.02 calls per day, with a standard deviation of 1.23 calls per day. At the .05 significance level, is there a difference in the mean number of calls per day between the two employees. What is the p-value? (Textbook Problem 11-25)

11-3. The Willow Run Outlet Mall has two Haggar Outlet Stores, one located on Peach Street and the other on Plum Street. The two stores are laid out differently, but both store managers claim their layout maximizes the amounts customers will purchase on impulse. A sample of ten customers at the Peach Street store revealed they spent the following amounts more than planned: $17.58, $19.73, $12.61, $17.79, $16.22, $15.82, $15.40, $15.86, $11.82, $15.85. A sample of fourteen customers at the Plum Street store revealed they spent the following amounts more than they planned when they entered the store: $18.19, $20.22, $17.38, $17.96, $23.92, $15.87, $16.47, $15.96, $16.79, $16.74, $21.40, $20.57, $19.79, $14.83. At the .01 significance level is there a difference in the mean amount purchased on an impulse at the two stores? (Textbook Problem 11-35)

11-4. The owner of Bun N Run Hamburger wishes to compare the sales per day at two locations. The mean number sold for 10 randomly selected days at the Northside site was 83.55, and the standard deviation was 10.50. For a random sample of 12 days at the Southside location, the mean number sold was 78.80 and the standard deviation was 14.25. At the .05 significance level, is there a difference in the mean number of hamburgers sold at the two locations? (Textbook Problem 11-33)

11-5. As part of a recent survey among dual-wage-earner couples, an industrial psychologist found that 990 men out of the 1,500 surveyed believed that division of household duties was fair. A sample of 1,600 women found that 970 believed the division of household duties was fair. At the .01 significance level, is it reasonable to conclude that the proportion of men who believe the division of household duties is fair is larger? (Textbook Problem 11-31)

11-6. The federal government recently granted funds for a special program designed to reduce crime in high-crime areas. A study of the results of the program in eight high-crime areas of Miami, FL, yielded the following results. (Textbook Problem 11-22)

Number of Crimes by Area

	A	B	C	D	E	F	G	H
Before	14	7	4	5	17	12	8	9
After	2	7	3	6	8	13	3	5

Has there been a decrease in the number of crimes since the inauguration of the program? Use the .01 significance level.

11-7. Each month the National Association of Purchasing Managers publishes the NAPM index. One of the questions asked on the survey to purchasing agents is: Do you think the economy is expanding? Last month of the 300 responses, 160 answered the yes to the question. This month 170 of the 290 responses indicated they felt the economy was expanding. At the .05 significance level can we conclude that a larger proportion of the agents believe the economy is expanding this month? (Textbook Problem 11-30)

11-8. Two boats, the Prada (Italy) and the Oracle (USA), are competing for a spot in the upcoming America's Cup race. They race over a part of the course several times. Below are the sample times in minutes. At the .05 significance level, can we conclude that there is a difference in their mean times? (Textbook Problem 11-38)

Prada (Italy)	Oracle (USA)
12.9	14.1
12.5	14.1
11.0	14.2
13.3	17.4
11.2	15.8
11.4	16.7
11.6	16.1
12.3	13.3
14.2	13.4
11.3	13.6
	10.8
	19.0

11-9. A number of minor automobile accidents occur at various high-risk intersections in Teton County despite traffic lights. The traffic department claims that a modification in the type of light will reduce these accidents. The county commissioners have agreed to a proposed experiment. Eight intersections were chosen at random, and the lights at those intersections were modified. The numbers of minor accidents during a six-month period before and after the modifications were: (Textbook Problem 11-40)

	Number of accidents, by intersection							
	A	B	C	D	E	F	G	H
Before modification	5	7	6	4	8	9	8	10
After modification	3	7	7	0	4	6	8	2

At the .01 significance level is it reasonable to conclude that the modification reduced the number of traffic accidents?

CHAPTER
12
ANALYSIS OF VARIANCE

CHAPTER GOALS

After completing this chapter, you will be able to:

1. List the characteristics of the F distribution.

2. Discuss the general idea of analysis of variance.

3. Use Excel to conduct a hypothesis test to determine if two sample variances came from similar populations.

4. Use Excel to set up and organize data into an ANOVA table.

5. Use Excel to conduct a test for differences among three or more treatment means.

6. Use Excel to conduct a test of hypothesis to determine if there is a difference between block means.

Introduction

In this chapter we will continue to discuss hypothesis testing by introducing the F distribution. The F distribution is used as the test statistic for several situations. It is used to test whether two samples are from populations having equal variances, and it is also applied when we want to compare more than two population means simultaneously. The simultaneous comparison of several population means is called **analysis of variance (ANOVA).** In both of these situations, the populations must be normal, and the data must be at least interval-scale.

Characteristics of the F Distribution

- There is a "family" of F distributions. A particular member of the family is determined by two parameters: the degrees of freedom in the numerator and the degrees of freedom in the denominator.

- F cannot be negative, and it is a continuous distribution.

- The curve representing an F distribution is positively skewed.

- It is asymptotic. Its values range from 0 to infinity. As the values of F increases, the curve approaches the X-axis, but it never touches it.

Steps in hypothesis testing:

1. **State the null and alternative hypothesis** using either formulas or words.
   The Null Hypothesis (H_o) is always the statement of no significant difference.

   The Alternative Hypothesis (H_1) is always the statement that there is a significant difference. When direction is stated it is a one-directional test (one-tailed). When direction is not stated it is a two-directional test (two-tailed).

2. **State the level of significance** or the probability that the null hypothesis is rejected when, in fact, it is true.

3. **State the statistical test** you will be using: the z test, t test, F test, Chi Square test, etc.

4. **Formulate a decision rule**. Using a picture or curve that estimates the distribution you are testing, show the critical value if you are performing a one-directional test or the upper and lower critical values if you are performing a two-directional test.

5. **Do it**. Show the formula you used and at least the major steps involved. State the results of the hypothesis test in terms of the question using complete sentences and examples.

F-Test Two-Sample for Variances

Excel has a data analysis program for finding an F-test for two sample variances.

Example 1. The production supervisor at Corry Steel Company, a manufacturer of steel desks, wants to compare the number of defective desks produced on the day shift versus the number produced on the afternoon shift. A sample of the production from 6 day shifts and 8 afternoon shifts revealed the following information:

Day	5	8	7	6	9	7		
Afternoon	8	10	7	11	9	12	14	9

At the .05 significance level, is the variance of the number of defects in the afternoon shift greater than the variance of the number of defects in the day shift?

1. In a new worksheet, key the data as shown.

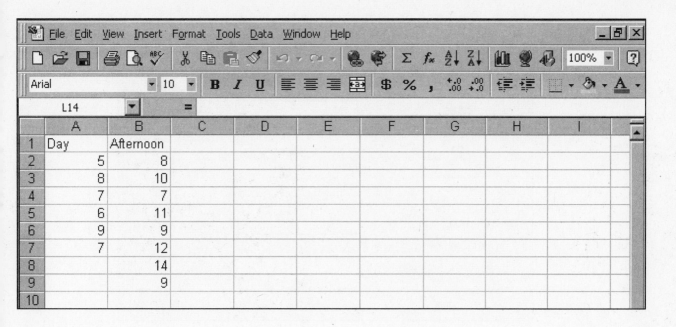

From the **Menu bar,** select **T**ools. If Data Analysis does not appear, select **Add-I**ns. Select **Analysis ToolPak.** Click OK.

2. From the **Menu bar,** select **T**ools. Select **D**ata Analysis. Select **F-Test Two Sample for Variances.** Click OK.

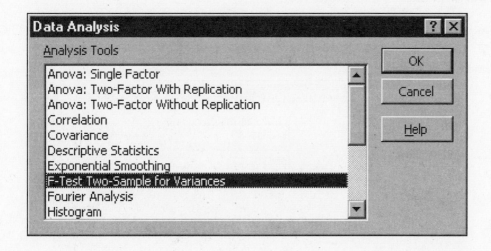

The dialog box for F-Test Two-Sample for Variances, is displayed.

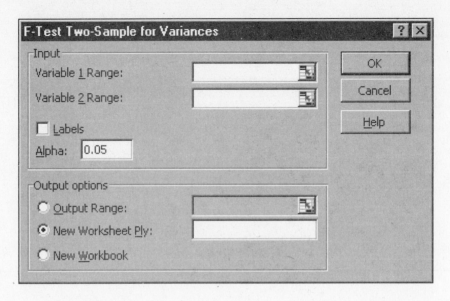

3. Your cursor should be on the Variable 1 Range text box. Key **A1:A7**. Touch the **tab** key.

4. In the Variable 2 Range text box, key **B1:B9**. Touch the **tab** key.

5. Select Labels, check box. Touch the **tab** key.

6. The Alpha text box should have **.05**.

7. Select Output Range, check box. In the Output Range text box, key **D1**. Click OK.

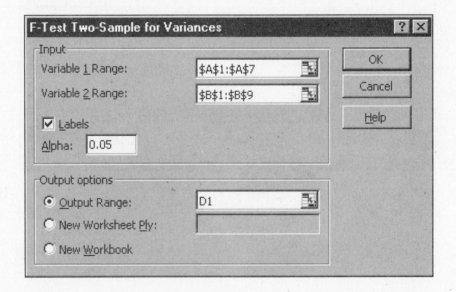

The output box is displayed but is difficult to read.

	A	B	C	D	E	F	G	H	I
1	Day	Afternoon		F-Test Two-Sample for Variances					
2	5	8							
3	8	10			Day	Afternoon			
4	7	7		Mean	7	10			
5	6	11		Variance	2	5.142857			
6	9	9		Observatio	6	8			
7	7	12		df	5	7			
8		14		F	0.388889				
9		9		P(F<=f) on	0.157896				
10				F Critical c	0.205091				
11									

8. Make D10 your active cell. From the Menu bar, select Format. Select Column. Select AutoFit selection.

	A	B	C	D	E	F	G	H	I
1	Day	Afternoon		F-Test Two-Sample for Variances					
2	5	8							
3	8	10			Day	Afternoon			
4	7	7		Mean	7	10			
5	6	11		Variance	2	5.142857			
6	9	9		Observations	6	8			
7	7	12		df	5	7			
8		14		F	0.388889				
9		9		P(F<=f) one-tail	0.157896				
10				F Critical one-tail	0.205091				
11									

Your table in now easier to read and can be interpreted.

The null hypothesis is rejected at the .05 level because the computed value for F .388889 is greater than the critical value of .205091. The variance of the defects in the afternoon shift is greater than the variance of the defects in the day shift.

If you wish, save your file as **ex1-var**. Close your file.

Single Factor Analysis of Variance

Excel has a data analysis program for finding analysis of variance (ANOVA).

Example 2. The manager of a computer software company is studying the number of hours top executives spend at their computer terminals by type of industry. A sample of five executives from each of three industries is obtained. At the .05 significance level, can the manager conclude there is a difference in the mean number of hours spent at a terminal per week by industry?

Banking	Retail	Insurance
12	8	10
10	8	8
10	6	6
12	8	8
10	10	10

At the .05 significance level, is there a difference in the mean scores?

1. In a new worksheet, key the data as shown below.

	A	B	C	D	E	F	G	H	I
1	Banking	Retail	Insurance						
2	12	8	10						
3	10	8	8						
4	10	6	6						
5	12	8	8						
6	10	10	10						
7									

From the Menu bar, select Tools. If Data Analysis does not appear, select Add-Ins. Select Analysis ToolPak. Click OK.

2. From the Menu bar, select Tools. Select Data Analysis. Select Anova: Single Factor. Click OK.

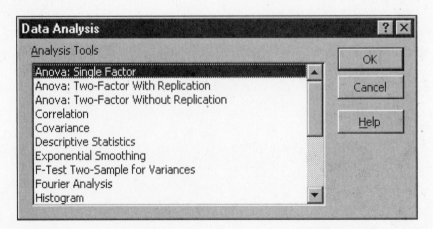

The dialog box for Anova: Single Factor, is displayed.

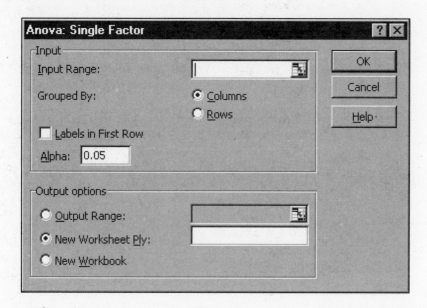

3. Your cursor should be on the Input Range text box. Key **A1:C6**. Touch the tab key.

4. Grouped by Columns should be selected. Touch the tab key.

5. Select Labels in First Row, check box. Touch the tab key.

6. The Alpha text box should have .05

7. Select Output Range, check box. In the Output Range text box, key **A8**. Click OK.

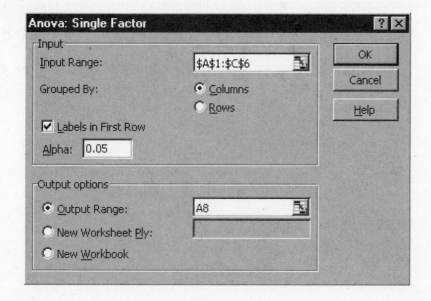

The output box is now displayed but it is difficult to read.

	A	B	C	D	E	F	G	H	I
1	Banking	Retail	Insurance						
2	12	8	10						
3	10	8	8						
4	10	6	6						
5	12	8	8						
6	10	10	10						
7									
8	Anova: Single Factor								
9									
10	SUMMARY								
11	Groups	Count	Sum	Average	Variance				
12	Banking	5	54	10.8	1.2				
13	Retail	5	40	8	2				
14	Insurance	5	42	8.4	2.8				
15									
16									
17	ANOVA								
18	rce of Varia	SS	df	MS	F	P-value	F crit		
19	Between G	22.93333	2	11.46667	5.733333	0.01788	3.88529		
20	Within Gro	24	12	2					
21									
22	Total	46.93333	14						
23									

8. Make A18 your active cell. From the Menu bar, select Format. Select Column. Select AutoFit selection.

	A	B	C	D	E	F	G	H
1	Banking	Retail	Insurance					
2	12	8	10					
3	10	8	8					
4	10	6	6					
5	12	8	8					
6	10	10	10					
7								
8	Anova: Single Factor							
9								
10	SUMMARY							
11	Groups	Count	Sum	Average	Variance			
12	Banking	5	54	10.8	1.2			
13	Retail	5	40	8	2			
14	Insurance	5	42	8.4	2.8			
15								
16								
17	ANOVA							
18	Source of Variation	SS	df	MS	F	P-value	F crit	
19	Between Groups	22.93333	2	11.46667	5.733333	0.01788	3.88529	
20	Within Groups	24	12	2				
21								
22	Total	46.93333	14					
23								

Your table is now easier to read and can be interpreted.

The computed F of 5.733333 is greater than the F critical value of 3.88529 so we reject the null hypothesis. There is a difference in the mean number of hours spent at a terminal per week by industry.

If you wish, save your file as **ex2-var**. Close your file.

Two Factor Analysis of Variance

Example 3. Rudduck Shampoo sells three shampoos: for dry, normal, and oily hair. Sales, in millions of dollars, for the past five months are given in the following table.

Sales ($millions)

Month	Dry	Normal	Oily
June	7	9	12
July	11	12	14
August	13	11	8
September	8	9	7
October	9	10	13

Using the .05 level, apply the ANOVA procedure to test whether:

a. The mean sales for dry, normal, and oily hair are the same.

b. The mean sales are the same for each of the five months.

1. In a new worksheet, key the data as shown above.

	A	B	C	D	E	F	G	H	I
1	Month	Dry	Normal	Oily					
2	June	7	9	12					
3	July	11	12	14					
4	August	13	11	8					
5	September	8	9	7					
6	October	9	10	13					
7									

From the Menu bar, select Tools. If Data Analysis does not appear, select Add-Ins. Select Analysis ToolPak. Click OK.

2. From the Menu bar, select Tools. Select Data Analysis. Select Anova: Two-Factor Without Replication. Click OK.

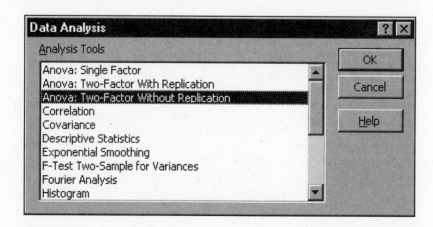

The dialog box for Anova: Two Factor Without Replication looks similar to the single factor dialog box.

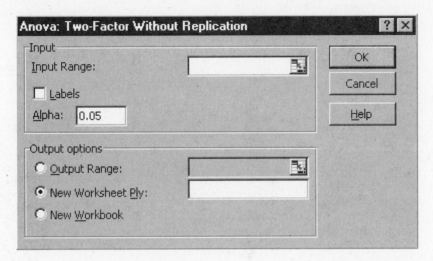

3. Your cursor should be on the Input Range text box. Key **A1:D6**. Touch the tab key.

4. Select Labels check box. Touch the tab key.

5. The Alpha text box should have .05

6. Select Output Range, check box. In the Output Range text box, key **A8**. Click OK.

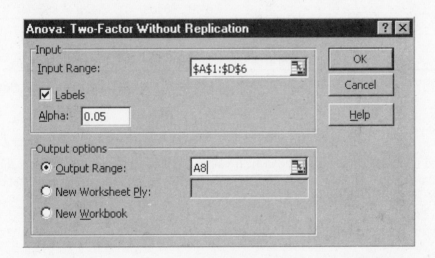

7. Make A23 your active cell. From the Menu bar, select Format. Select Column. Select AutoFit Selection.

	A	B	C	D	E	F	G	H
1	Month	Dry	Normal	Oily				
2	June	7	9	12				
3	July	11	12	14				
4	August	13	11	8				
5	September	8	9	7				
6	October	9	10	13				
7								
8	Anova: Two-Factor Without Replication							
9								
10	SUMMARY	Count	Sum	Average	Variance			
11	June	3	28	9.333333	6.333333			
12	July	3	37	12.33333	2.333333			
13	August	3	32	10.66667	6.333333			
14	September	3	24	8	1			
15	October	3	32	10.66667	4.333333			
16								
17	Dry	5	48	9.6	5.8			
18	Normal	5	51	10.2	1.7			
19	Oily	5	54	10.8	9.7			
20								
21								
22	ANOVA							
23	Source of Variation	SS	df	MS	F	P-value	F crit	
24	Rows	31.73333	4	7.933333	1.71223	0.239694	3.837854	
25	Columns	3.6	2	1.8	0.388489	0.690208	4.458968	
26	Error	37.06667	8	4.633333				
27								
28	Total	72.4	14					
29								

Your table is displayed and can be interpreted.

Since the computed F values are less than the critical values, we accept the null hypothesis for both rows and columns. At the .05 level there is not a significant difference in the sales of the three types of shampoo, nor in the shampoo sales for different months.

If you wish, save your file as **ex3-var**. Close your file.

Practice Exercises taken from textbook.

In addition to showing your printout, state the results of the hypothesis test in terms of the question using complete sentences and examples.

12-1. The Willow Run Outlet Mall has two Haggar Outlet Stores, one located on Peach Street and the other on Plum Street. The two stores are laid out differently, but both store managers claim their layout maximizes the amounts customers will purchase on impulse. A sample of ten customers at the Peach Street store revealed they spent the following amounts more than planned: $17.58, $19.73, $12.61, $17.79, $16.22, $15.82, $15.40, $15.86, $11.82, $15.85. A sample of fourteen customers at the Plum Street store revealed they spent the following amounts more than they planned when they entered the store: $18.19, $20.22, $17.38, $17.96, $23.92, $15.87, $16.47, $15.96, $16.79, $16.74, $21.40, $20.57, $19.79, $14.83. At the .01 significance level is the variance of the Peach Street store greater than the variance of the Plum Street store?

12-2. There are two Chevy Dealers in Jamestown, NY. The mean weekly sales at Sharkey Chevy and Dave White Chevrolet are about the same. However, Tom Sharkey, the owner of Sharkey Chevy, believes his sales are more consistent. Below is the number of new cars sold at Sharkey in the last seven months, and for the last eight months at Dave White. Do you agree with Mr. Sharkey? Use the .01 significance level. (Textbook Problem 12-21) Hint: Use variable 1 as Dave White and variable 2 as Sharkey.

Sharkey					Dave White			
98	78	54	57		75	81	81	30
68	64	70			82	46	58	101

12-3. A consumer organization wants to know if there is a difference in the price of a particular toy at three different types of stores. The price of the toy was checked in a sample of five discount toy stores, five variety stores, and five department stores. The results are shown below. (Textbook Problem 12-25)

Discount toy	Variety	Department
$12	15	19
13	17	17
14	14	16
12	18	20
15	17	19

Use the .05 significance level to conduct the test.

12-4. A physician who specializes in weight control has three different diets she recommends. As an experiment, she randomly selected 15 patients and then assigned 5 to each diet. After three weeks the following weight losses, in pounds, were noted. At the .05 significance level, can she conclude that there is a difference in the mean amount of weight loss among the three diets? (Textbook Problem 12-26)

Plan A	Plan B	Plan C
5	6	7
7	7	8
4	7	9
5	5	8
4	6	9

12-5. Martin Motors has in stock three cars of the same make and model. The president would like to compare the gas consumption of the three cars (labeled car A, car B, and car C) using four different types of gasoline. For each trial, a gallon of gasoline was added to an empty tank, and the car was driven until it ran out of gas. The following table shows the number of miles driven in each trial. (Textbook Problem 12-38)

Types of gasoline	Distance (miles)		
	Car A	Car B	Car C
Regular	22.4	20.8	21.5
Super	17.0	19.4	20.7
Unleaded	19.2	20.2	21.2
Premium unleaded	20.3	18.6	20.4

Using the .05 level of significance:
a. Is there a difference among types of gasoline?
b. Is there a difference in the cars?

12-6. There are four McBurger restaurants in the Columbus, Georgia, area. The numbers of burgers sold at the respective restaurants for each of the last six weeks are shown below. At the .05 significance level, is there a difference in the mean number sold among the four restaurants, when the factor of week is considered? (Textbook Problem 12-36)

		Restaurant		
Week	Metro	Interstate	University	River
1	124	160	320	190
2	234	220	340	230
3	430	290	290	240
4	105	245	310	170
5	240	205	280	180
6	310	260	270	205

a. Is there a difference is the treatment means?
b. Is there a difference in the block means?

CHAPTER
13
LINEAR REGRESSION AND CORRELATION

CHAPTER GOALS

After completing this chapter, you will be able to:

1. Explain correlation and regression.

2. Use Excel to draw a scatter diagram.

3. Use Excel to calculate the coefficient of determination.

4. Use Excel to find a least squares regression line.

5. Use Excel and the least squares regression equation to predict the value of a dependent variable based on an independent variable.

Introduction

The emphasis in this chapter is studying the relationship between two numbers and developing an equation that allows us to estimate one variable based on another. Is there a relationship between the temperature and the number of people on the beach? Is there a relationship between education and monthly earnings? Can we predict our grade on the next statistics test based on how much time we spend studying the material on the test?

Correlation analysis is a group of statistical techniques used to measure the strength of the relationship (correlation) between two variables. The **dependent variable**, the variable being predicted or estimated is shown on the vertical axis (Y-axis) and the **independent variable**, the predictor variable which provides the basis for estimation is shown on the horizontal axis (X-axis). The **coefficient of correlation** may assume any value on a scale of -1 to +1, inclusive. It describes the strength of the relationship between two sets of interval-scaled or ratio-scaled variables. A correlation coefficient of -1 or +1 indicates a perfect correlation. A coefficient of correlation close to 0 shows a weak relationship.

Terms such as weak, moderate, and strong, however, do not have precise meaning. A measure that has a more exact meaning is the **coefficient of determination**. It is computed by squaring the coefficient of correlation. The coefficient of determination is the total variation in the dependent variable Y that is explained, or accounted, for by the variation in the independent variable X.

Regression analysis is a technique used to express the relationship between two variables that estimates the value of the dependent variable Y based on a selected value of the independent variable X. The **least squares regression equation** ($Y = a + bX$) is the mathematical equation that defines the relationship between two variables that have a linear relationship.

a   is the estimated value of the dependent variable Y where the regression line crosses the Y-axis when X is zero.

b   is the slope of the line, or the average change in *Y* for each change of one unit (either increase or decrease) in the independent variable X.

The following examples show how you can use Excel to work with correlation and regression analysis:

Like chapter 4 we will use Excel to plot a scatter diagram. In this chapter we will add a least squares regression line which will be used to help determine a coefficient of determination. Then we will develop a regression equation to use in predicting a dependent value, given the independent value.

Scatter Diagrams and Least Squares Regression Line

Example 1. Reliable Furniture is a family business that has been selling to retail customers in the Chicago area for many years. They advertise extensively on radio and TV emphasizing their low prices and easy credit terms. The owner would like to review the relationship between sales (in millions of dollars) and the amount spent on advertising (in millions of dollars). Below is information on sales and advertising expense for the last four months.

Month	Advertising expense ($million)	Sales revenue ($million)
July	2	4
August	1	3
September	3	8
October	4	10

The owner wants to forecast sales based on advertising expense.

a. Draw a scatter diagram with a least squares regression line.

b. What is the coefficient of determination?

c. Assuming a normal distribution, using the regression equation, (1) estimate the revenue for an advertising expense of 1.5 million dollars, (2) estimate the revenue for an advertising expense of 3.5 million dollars.

Creating a scatter diagram with a least squares regression line.

NOTE: When entering the data you <u>must</u> put the data for the independent variable **first**.

1. On a new worksheet, enter the data for the problem as shown below. Notice that the data for Advertising is entered first since it is the independent variable.

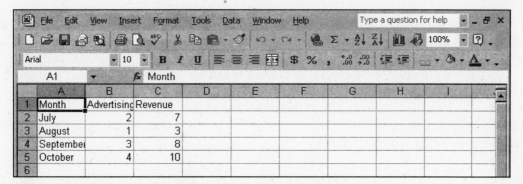

2. Highlight **B1:C5**. From the Tool bar select ChartWizard.

3. In Step 1, under Chart type, select XY (Scatter). Under Chart sub-type, the upper left chart should be selected. Click Next.

4. In Step 2, Accept the defaults. Click Next.

5. In Step 3, at the top, the Titles tab should be selected. Click on the Chart title text box, key **Correlation Between Advertising and Revenue**. Tab to the Value (X) axis text box. Key **Advertising**. Tab to the Value (Y) axis text box. Key **Revenue**.

6. At the top, select the Legend tab. Click in the Show legend check box to de-select the legend. Click Finish.

The condensed scatter chart is formed.

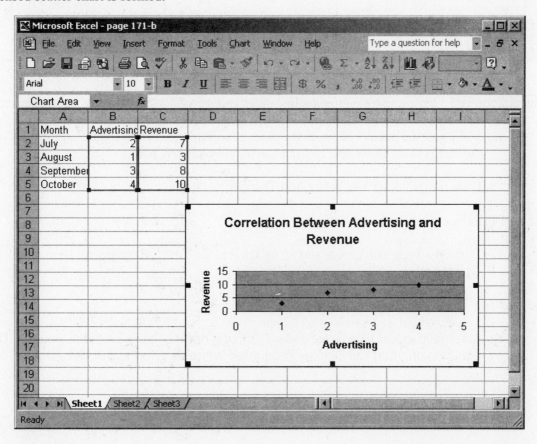

7. With the handles still on the chart, click and hold the left mouse button inside the chart. A 4-way arrow will show in the chart. As you move the chart it will show as an open box with dashed lines. With your mouse button still depressed, drag your mouse and move your chart so the left edge of the chart is in column D and the top edge of the chart is in row 2.

8. Click on the bottom handle of the chart. Drag the bottom line to row 16.

The chart is now larger and easier to read.

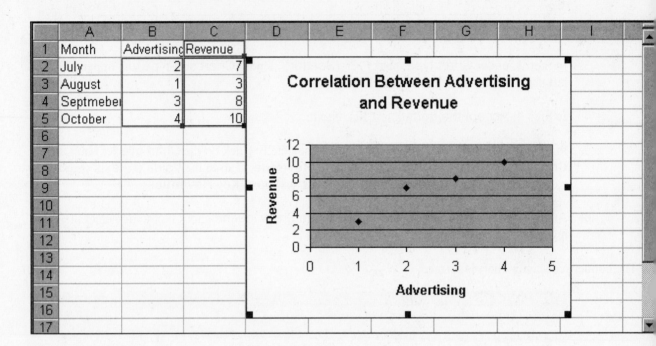

You will now add a least squares regression line or a *trendline*.

9. Make sure the handles show on the chart box. With your **right** mouse arrow, click on one of the data points. There will be a dot inserted in each data point.

10. From the pull down list, select Add T<u>r</u>endline.

The Add Trendline dialog box appears.

11. Under the Type tab, <u>L</u>inear should be selected for Trend/Regression type. Click on the Options tab.

The Add Trendline Options dialog box appears.

12. <u>A</u>utomatic should be selected under Trendline name. Select the check boxes for Display <u>e</u>quation on chart and Display <u>R</u>-squared value on chart. Click OK.

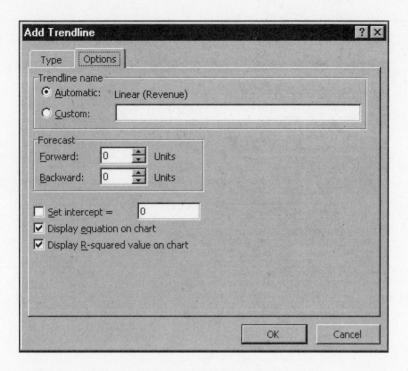

The regression equation and R^2 are shown, but hard to read.

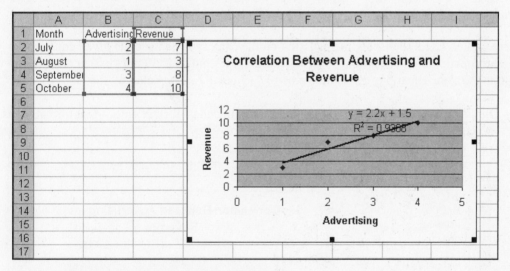

13. Click anywhere on the equation. A shadow box appears around the outside. Place your arrow on any line. Your mouse arrow will remain as an arrow. Click, hold and drag the box next to the word Revenue.

The equation y=2.2x +1.5 and $R^2 = 0.9308$ is now off the chart and is easier to read.

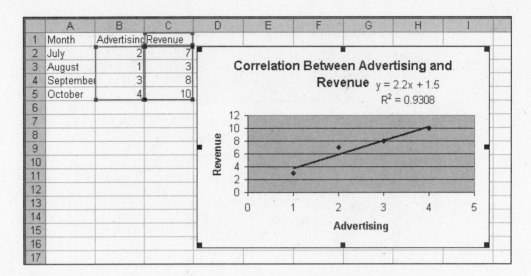

Example 2. Since you requested Excel to display the R^2 value on the chart, you can read from the chart that the coefficient of determination is .9308.

On the same worksheet containing your chart, in A7, key **Coeffic of determ = .9308**.

Example 3. You will use the regression equation to estimate the revenue based on the amount spent on advertising (x). The equation is $Y' = a + bX$, or $y = bx + a$ as used in Excel.

Since you requested Excel to display the equation on the chart, you can use the given equation for your estimate. The equation on the chart uses "y" instead of " Y' " and has "a" and "bx" in reverse order, but otherwise it is the same equation. 1.5 is the value of "a" and 2.2 is the value of "b".

1. On the same worksheet containing your chart, in cells A9:B12, enter the information as shown.

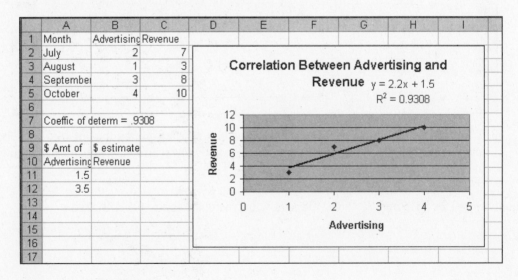

2. In B11, key =**1.5+2.2*A11**

3. Copy B11 to B12.

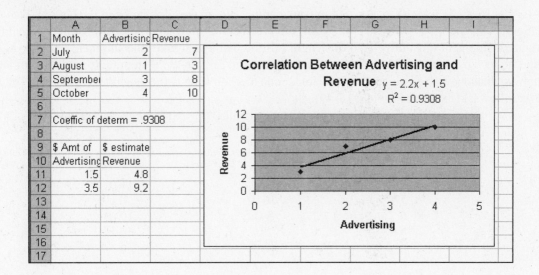

This computes the estimated revenue for both amounts of advertising and completes your problem.

If you wish, save your file as **linreg-1**. Close your file.

Practice Exercises taken from textbook.

13-1. The Bardi Trucking Co., located in Cleveland, Ohio, makes deliveries in the Great Lakes region, the Southeast, and the Northeast. Jim Bardi, the president, is studying the relationship between the distance a shipment must travel and the length of time, in days, it takes the shipment to arrive at its destination. To investigate, Mr. Bardi selected a random sample of 20 shipments made last month. Shipping distance is the independent variable, and shipping time is the dependent variable. The results are as follows. (Textbook Problem 13-49)

Shipment	Distance (miles)	Shipping time (days)
1	656	5
2	853	14
3	646	6
4	783	11
5	610	8
6	841	10
7	785	9
8	639	9
9	762	10
10	762	9
11	862	7
12	679	5
13	835	13
14	607	3
15	665	8
16	647	7
17	685	10
18	720	8
19	652	6
20	828	10

a. Determine and interpret the coefficient of determination.
b. What would be the estimated shipping time for a distance of 715 miles?

13-2. A sample of 12 homes sold last week in St Paul, Minnesota, is selected. The results are shown below. (Textbook Problem 13-42)

Home Size (thousands of square feet)	Selling price ($thousands)	Home Size (thousands of square feet)	Selling price ($thousands)
1.4	100	1.3	110
1.3	110	0.8	85
1.2	105	1.2	105
1.1	120	0.9	75
1.4	80	1.1	70
1.0	105	1.1	95

a. Determine and interpret the coefficient of determination.
b. What would be the estimated selling price of a home that has 1.0 thousand square feet?

CHAPTER
14
MULTIPLE REGRESSION AND CORRELATION ANALYSIS

After completing this chapter, you will be able to:

1. Explain multiple regression and correlation.

2. Use Excel to calculate the multiple coefficient of determination.

3. Use Excel to describe the relationship between two or more independent variables and a dependent variable using a multiple regression equation.

4. Use Excel and the least squares regression equation to predict the value of a dependent variable based on two or more independent variables.

Introduction

Chapter 13 explained regression and correlation analysis, which allowed us to estimate one variable based on another. The use of only one independent variable to predict the dependent variable ignores the relationship of other variables to the dependent variable. This chapter expands the concept by allowing us to use more than one explanatory variable in a regression equation. Using more than one independent variable makes it possible to increase the explanatory power and the usefulness of regression and correlation analysis in making many business decisions.

This chapter shows you how to use Excel to find a multiple regression equation, predict a dependent variable based on two or more independent variables and find the multiple coefficient of determination.

The following example will show how you can use Excel to work with multiple regression and correlation.

Multiple Regression and Correlation.

The multiple regression model allows one to predict the value of a dependent variable by incorporating two or more independent variables.

The textbook states the estimated multiple regression model as $Y' = a + b_1X_1 + b_2X_2 + \ldots b_kX_k$. Excel uses the "least squares" method to calculate a straight line that best fits the data and returns an array that describes the line. The multiple regression equation for the line is: $y = m_1x_1 + m_2x_2 + \ldots m_nx_n + b$.

You will use the LINEST function of Excel. LINEST gives you the means to predict the dependent variable and the coefficient of determination.

The LINEST function is written, **=LINEST(known_y's,known_x's,const,stats)** , where:

known_y's is the range of y-values you already know

known_x's is the range of the known variables

const is a logical whether or not to calculate the constant normally. For these problems it will always be TRUE.

stats is a logical value specifying whether to return additional regression statistics such as the coefficient of determination. Since you want the additional statistics, it will always be TRUE.

The *array* that LINEST *returns* is $\{m_n, m_{n-1},...m_1, b\}$. So the coefficients that correspond to each x-value in the array are the **reverse** of the coefficients in the multiple regression equation for the line. When entering the data into Excel, you must enter the data for the independent variables **first**, then your known Y values.

Example. The quality control engineer at Bethel Steel is interested in estimating the tensile strength of steel wire based on its outside diameter and the amount of molybdenum in the steel. As an experiment, she selected four pieces of wire, measured the outside diameters, and determined the molybdenum content. Then she measured the tensile strength of each piece. The results were:

Piece	Tensile Strength (psi) Y	Outside diameter (cm) X1	Amount of molybdenum (units) X2
A	11	3	6
B	9	2	5
C	16	4	8
D	12	3	7

Using a multiple regression equation, what is the estimated tensile strength of a steel wire having an outside diameter of 3.5 cm and 6.4 units of molybdenum? What is the multiple coefficient of determination?

You will use the LINEST function to calculate coefficients needed in the multiple regression to predict the tensile strength of the steel wire. Notice the independent variables of X2 and X1 were entered first, then the known Y values. In the multiple regression line, Excel reverses the order of the coefficients from the way they were listed in the worksheet. If you enter the independent variables in reverse order they will be correct in the multiple regression equation.

1. On a new worksheet, enter the data as shown.

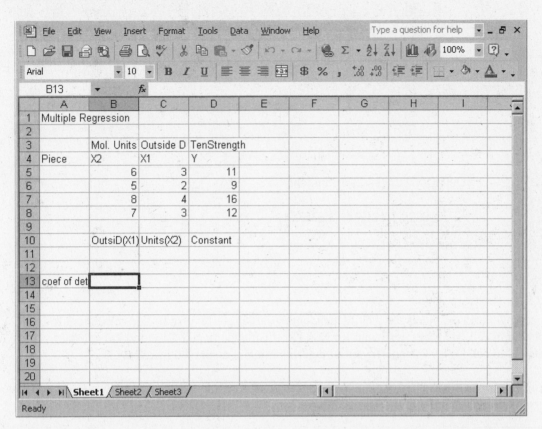

Notice that where the answers will be displayed, you place the coefficients in reverse order of the way they were entered on the worksheet. The LINEST function always displays the constant value last. **Be sure** when you key the LINEST function you list the cell contents for the known **Y values first**.

2. Highlight **B11:D13**. With the range still highlighted, key
   =LINEST(D5:D8,B5:C8,TRUE,TRUE) DO NOT TOUCH THE <ENTER> KEY YET!

3. After you have finished keying, hold down the <Shift> key and the <Ctrl> key together and at the same time touch the <Enter> key. The formula in the formula bar at the top of the worksheet should be inside curly brackets, {}.

	A	B	C	D	E	F	G	H	I
1	Multiple Regression								
2									
3		Mol. Units	Outside D	TenStrength					
4	Piece	X2	X1	Y					
5	A	6	3	11					
6	B	5	2	9					
7	C	8	4	16					
8	D	7	3	12					
9									
10		OutsiD(X1)	Units(X2)	Constant					
11		2	1	-0.5					
12		2.236068	1.414214	3.570714					
13	coef of det	0.961538	1	#N/A					
14									

Notice how the coefficients for the independent variables are reversed. The coefficient for X1 (2) is displayed in cell B11, the coefficient for X2 (1) is displayed in cell C11, and the constant value (-0.5) is displayed in cell D11. The coefficient of determination is displayed in cell B13.

Always highlight 3 rows before you key your LINEST function. In the Excel output, the coefficient of determination will be the first cell in the third row.

Using row 11, you can construct a multiple regression equation to predict the tensile strength of the wire (Y)

Y = -0.5 + 2 (Outside D) + 1 (mol units)

> 4. In A15 to A17, key respectively, **Outside Diameter(X1)=**, **Molybdenum units(X2)=**, **Predicted Tensile strength(Y)=**
>
> 5. In D15, key **3.5**, in D16, key **6.4**, in D17, key **=D11+D15*B11+D16*C11**

This gives you the estimated tensile strength of 12.9. If you want to experiment to see what the predicted tensile strength would be for different values of the Outside Diameter and the Molybdenum units, you can key in other values for cells D15 and D16.

	A	B	C	D	E	F	G	H	I
3		Mol. Units	Outside D	TenStrength					
4	Piece	X2	X1	Y					
5	A	6	3	11					
6	B	5	2	9					
7	C	8	4	16					
8	D	7	3	12					
9									
10		OutsiD(X1)	Units(X2)	Constant					
11		2	1	-0.5					
12		2.236068	1.414214	3.570714					
13	coef of det	0.961538	1	#N/A					
14									
15	Outside Diameter(X1)=			3.5					
16	Molybdenum units(X2)=			6.4					
17	Predicted Tensil strength(Y)=			12.9					
18									

Use Excel's LINEST function to construct the multiple regression equation for the following problems, and use the equation to make predictions.

Practice Exercises taken from the textbook.

14-1. Suppose that the sales manager of a large automotive parts distributor wants to estimate as early as April, the total annual sales of a region. Based on regional sales, the total sales for the company can also be estimated. If, based on past experience, it is found that the April estimates of annual sales are reasonably accurate, then in future years the April forecast could be used to revise production schedules and maintain the correct inventory at the retail outlets.

Several factors appear to be related to sales, including the number of retail outlets in the region stocking the company's parts, the number of automobiles in the region registered as of April 1, and the total personal income for the first quarter of the year. A total of five independent variables were finally selected as being the most important (according to the sales manager). Then the data were gathered for a recent year. The total annual sales for the year for each region were also recorded. Note in the following table that for region 1 there were 1.139 retail outlets stocking the company's automotive parts, there were 9,270,000 registered automobiles in the region as of April 1, and sales for that year were $37,702,000. (Textbook Problem 14-14)

Annual Sales ($ millions) Y	Number of retail outlets, X1	Number automobiles registered (millions) X2	Personal income ($ billions) X3	Average age of automobiles (years) X4	Number of supervisors X5
37.702	1739	9.27	85.4	3.5	9.0
24.196	1221	5.86	60.7	5.0	5.0
32.055	1646	8.81	68.1	4.4	7.0
3.611	120	3.81	20.2	4.0	5.0
17.625	1096	10.31	33.8	3.5	7.0
45.919	2290	11.62	95.1	4.1	13.0
29.600	1687	8.96	69.3	4.1	15.0
8.114	241	6.28	16.3	5.9	11.0
20.116	649	7.77	34.9	5.5	16.0
12.994	1427	10.92	15.1	4.1	10.0

What are the predicted Annual sales for 1,946 retail outlets, 8.65 million registered automobiles, Personal income of 93.2 billion, average age of automobile of 4.8 years, and Number of supervisors 12?

HINT: On your worksheet, list Annual sales last and the independent variables beginning with X5. Be sure to highlight 3 rows and 6 columns before you type your LINEST function.

14-2. The administrator of a new paralegal program at Seagate Technical College wants to estimate the grade point average in the new program. He thought that high school GPA, the verbal score on the Scholastic Aptitude Test (SAT), and the mathematics score on the SAT would be good predictors of paralegal GPA. The data on nine students are: (Textbook Problem 14-15)

Student	High school GPA	SAT verbal	SAT math	Paralegal GPA
1	3.25	480	410	3.21
2	1.80	290	270	1.68
3	2.89	420	410	3.58
4	3.81	500	600	3.92
5	3.13	500	490	3.00
6	2.81	430	460	2.82
7	2.20	320	490	1.65
8	2.14	530	480	3.30
9	2.63	469	440	2.33

What is the predicted Paralegal GPA for a High school GPA of 3.53, a verbal SAT of 560, and a math SAT of 450?

HINT: On your worksheet, list Paralegal GPA last and the independent variables beginning with the math SAT. Be sure to highlight 3 rows and 4 columns before you type your LINEST function.

CHAPTER
15
NONPARAMETRIC METHODS: CHI-SQUARE APPLICATIONS

CHAPTER GOALS

After completing this chapter, you will be able to:

1. List the characteristics of the chi-square distribution along with some of its uses and limitations.

2. Use Excel to conduct a goodness-of-fit test of hypothesis involving the difference between a set of observed frequencies and a corresponding set of expected frequencies.

3. Use Excel to conduct a contingency table analysis, a test of hypothesis to determine whether two criteria of classification are related.

Introduction

Chapters 10 through 12 dealt with data that were at least interval-scale, such as weights, incomes, and ages. We conducted a number of tests of hypothesis about a population mean and two or more population means. For these tests it was assumed that the population was normal. This chapter deals with the **chi-square distribution**, hypothesis tests where the data does not need to be interval-scale, but could be nominal- or ordinal-scale, and where no assumptions are made about the shape of the parent population. This hypothesis test is called a **nonparametric test** or a **distribution-free test.**

Characteristics of the Chi-Square Distribution

- The computed value of chi-square is always positive because the difference between f_o and f_e is squared, that is, $(f_o - f_e)^2$.

- There is a family of chi-square distributions. There is a chi-square distribution for 1 degree of freedom, another for 2 degrees of freedom, another for 3 degrees of freedom, and so on. In this type of problem the number of degrees of freedom is determined by k-1, where k is the number of categories. Therefore, the shape of the chi-square distribution does not depend on the size of the sample. For example, if 300 employees of a school district were classified into one of three categories--support staff, teachers, and administration--there would be k-1 = 3-1=2 degrees of freedom.

- The chi-square distribution is positively skewed. However, as the number of degrees of freedom increases the distribution begins to approximate the normal distribution.

Limitations of Chi-Square

If there is an unusually small expected frequency in a cell, chi-square (if applied) might result in an erroneous conclusion. This can happen because f_e appears in the denominator, and dividing by a very small number makes the quotient quite large! Two generally accepted rules regarding small cell frequencies are:

☐☐ If there are only two cells, the expected frequency in each cell should be 5 or more.

☐☐ For more than two cells, chi-square should not be applied if more than 20 percent of the f_e cells have expected frequencies less than 5.

Use the same five steps in hypothesis testing that were used in Chapters 9 through 11:

Steps in hypothesis testing:

1. **State the null and alternative hypothesis** using either formulas or words. The null hypothesis (H_o) is always the statement of no significant difference.

   The alternative hypothesis (H_1) is always the statement that there is a significant difference. When direction is stated it is a one-directional test (one-tailed). When direction is not stated it is a two-directional test (two-tailed).

2. **State the level of significance** or the probability that the null hypothesis is rejected when, in fact, it is true.

3. **State the statistical test** you will be using: the z test, t test, F test, chi square test, etc.

4. **Formulate a decision rule**. Using a picture or curve that estimates the distribution you are testing, show the critical value if you are performing a one-directional test or the upper and lower critical values if you are performing a two-directional test.

5. **Do it**. Show the formula you used and at least the major steps involved. State the results of the hypothesis test in terms of the question using complete sentences and examples.

Equal Expected Frequencies

In this chapter you will be working with the chi-square distribution. There is no worksheet that can be created that will fit all problems of a particular type. What follows are examples of different situations. You will need to modify the worksheets when doing other problems.

The formula for the test statistic of chi-square is $X^2 = \Sigma\left[\dfrac{(f_o - f_e)^2}{f_e}\right]$

This formula will be referred to as Chi_Sq.

f_o is an observed frequency in a particular situation. It will be referred to as fo.

f_e is an expected frequency in a particular situation. It will be referred to as fe.

You will also need the degrees of freedom for computing the critical value. Degrees of freedom will be referred to as df, the critical value will be referred to as Crit_Val.

The formula for degrees of freedom is df = k-1, where k is the number of categories or *cells*.

Example 1. The personnel manager is concerned about absenteeism. She decides to sample the records to determine if absenteeism is distributed evenly throughout the six-day workweek. The null hypothesis to be tested is: Absenteeism is distributed evenly throughout the week. The .01 level is to be used. The sample results are:

	Number absent
Monday	12
Tuesday	9
Wednesday	11
Thursday	10
Friday	9
Saturday	9

What does this indicate to the personnel manager?

    1. On a new worksheet, enter the data as shown on the next page.

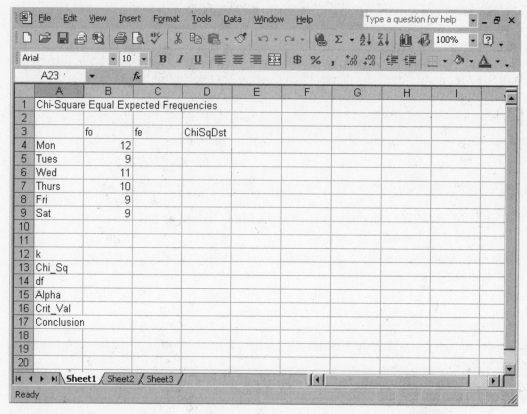

2. Highlight **A4:A16**. From the Tool bar, select Align Right button.

3. Highlight **B3:D9**. From the Menu bar select <u>I</u>nsert. Select <u>N</u>ame. Select <u>C</u>reate. Select <u>T</u>op Row. Click OK.

4. Highlight **A12:B16**. From the Menu bar select <u>I</u>nsert. Select <u>N</u>ame. Select <u>C</u>reate. Select <u>L</u>eft Column. Click OK.

5. In B12, key =**COUNT(fo)**

This will count the number of categories and give you the value of k.

6. In B13, key =**SUM(ChiSqDst)**

This will sum all the cell contents that you calculate.

7. In B14, key =**k-1**

8. In B15, key **.01**

9. In B16, key =**CHIINV(Alpha, df)**

This computes the critical value.

10. In B17, key =**IF(Chi_Sq>Crit_Val, "Reject Ho", "Do Not Reject Ho")**

As you are keying, your cell contents for A12:B17 will look as shown below.

	A	B	C	D	E	F	G	H	I
12	k	=COUNT(fo)							
13	Chi_Sq	=SUM(ChiSqDst)							
14	df	=k-1							
15	Alpha	0.01							
16	Crit_Val	=CHIINV(Alpha, df)							
17	Conclusion	=IF(Chi_Sq>Crit_Val, "Reject Ho", "Do Not Reject Ho")							
18									

11. In C4, key =**AVERAGE(fo)**

This is the expected frequency (f_e). This value will be copied to cells C5:C9.

12. In D4, key =**(fo-fe)^2/fe**

This is the square of each difference divided by the expected frequency. This formula will be copied to cells D5:D9.

The cell contents of C4 and D4 will look as shown below.

	A	B	C	D	E	F	G	H	I
1	Chi-Square Equal Expected Frequencies								
2									
3		fo	fe	ChiSqDst					
4	Mon	12	=AVERAGE(fo)	=(fo-fe)^2/fe					
5	Tues	9							
6	Wed	11							
7	Thurs	10							
8	Fri	9							
9	Sat	9							
10									

13. Highlight **C4:D4**. Place the mouse arrow on the lower right handle of D4. It will look like a thick black plus sign. Click and drag from D4:D9. This copies both the expected frequency and the formula and completes the table . Also, the remaining cells are computed and the output is complete.

	A	B	C	D	E	F	G	H	I
1	Chi-Square	Equal Expected Frequencies							
2									
3		fo	fe	ChiSqDst					
4	Mon	12	10	0.4					
5	Tues	9	10	0.1					
6	Wed	11	10	0.1					
7	Thurs	10	10	0					
8	Fri	9	10	0.1					
9	Sat	9	10	0.1					
10									
11									
12	k	6							
13	Chi_Sq	0.8							
14	df	5							
15	Alpha	0.01							
16	Crit_Val	15.08632							
17	Conclusion	Do Not Reject Ho							

The results can now be interpreted.

Do not reject Ho. The computed value for chi-square falls in the acceptance range because .8 is less than the critical value of 15.08632. Absenteeism is distributed evenly throughout the week. The observed differences are due to sampling variation.

Save your file as **chi-sqeq**. Close your file.

Example 2. To use this worksheet to solve other problems not having six categories, you must first rekey the category data in columns A and B. If you have less than 6 categories, you need to clear any cells in rows below the last category. If you have more than 6 categories you must copy the formulas for the extra rows in columns C and D. In both instances you then need to use the Name-Create function to rename columns B, C, and D using the new ranges. When you are asked if you would like to replace the existing definition, click on Yes. You may also need to key in a new value for Alpha.

In example 1, assume the business is also open on Sunday. You will modify the worksheet to include the extra category.

1. Open the file **chi-sqeq**.

2. In cells A10 and B10, key **Sun** and **13** respectively.

3. Highlight **C9:D9**. Drag the lower right handle of D9 to D10.

D10 reads #VALUE!, because cells B10 and C10 have no name.

4. Highlight **B3:D10**. Use the Name-Create function to rename the cells. In each instance when you are asked if you would like to replace the existing definition, click on Yes. You will be asked 3 times.

As soon as you are finished redefining columns B, C, and D, the output changes to reflect the new data.

	A	B	C	D	E	F	G	H	I
1	Chi-Square	Equal Expected Frequencies							
2									
3		fo	fe	ChiSqDst					
4	Mon	12	10.42857	0.236791					
5	Tues	9	10.42857	0.195695					
6	Wed	11	10.42857	0.031311					
7	Thurs	10	10.42857	0.017613					
8	Fri	9	10.42857	0.195695					
9	Sat	9	10.42857	0.195695					
10	Sun	13	10.42857	0.634051					
11									
12	k	7							
13	Chi_Sq	1.506849							
14	df	6							
15	Alpha	0.01							
16	Crit_Val	16.81187							
17	Conclusion	Do Not Reject Ho							

If you wish, save the file as **chi-sq2**. Close your file.

Contingency Tables

You will create a worksheet to determine expected frequencies when observed frequencies are known. You will also create a table to compute chi-square. You will create a worksheet to solve the following problem.

Example 3. A sociologist was researching this question: Is there any relationship between the level of education and social activities of an individual? She decided on three levels of education: attended or completed college, attended or completed high school, and attended or completed grade school or less. Each individual kept a record of his or her social activities, such as bowling with a group, dancing, and church functions. The sociologist divided them into above-average frequency, average frequency, and below-average frequency.

Social Activity

Education	Above average	Average	Below average
College	18	12	10
High school	17	15	13
Grade school	9	9	22

Can the sociologist conclude that there is no relationship between the level of education and the frequency of education?

    1. On a new worksheet, enter the data as shown below.

	A	B	C	D	E	F	G	H	I
1	Chi-Square Contingency Tables								
2									
3		Social Activity							
4	Education	AboveAvg	Average	BelowAvg	Total				
5	College								
6	High Sch								
7	Grade Sch								
8	Total					GrnTot			
9									

    2. Highlight **A3:E8**. From the Menu bar select <u>E</u>dit. Select <u>C</u>opy.

    3. Make A10 your active cell. From the Menu bar select <u>E</u>dit. Select <u>P</u>aste. Touch <Enter>.

    4. Highlight **A10:E15**. From the Menu bar select <u>E</u>dit. Select <u>C</u>opy.

    5. Make A17 your active cell. From the Menu bar select <u>E</u>dit. Select <u>P</u>aste. Touch <Enter>.

    6. In cell D3, key **(Observed)**

    7. In cell D10, key **(Expected)**

    8. In cell D17, key **(Chi-Square Computations)**

    9. In cells A24:A27, and B5:D7, enter the data as shown below.

	A	B	C	D	E	F	G	H	I
1	Chi-Square Contingency Tables								
2									
3		Social Activity		(Observed)					
4	Education	AboveAvg	Average	BelowAvg	Total				
5	College	18	12	10					
6	High Sch	17	15	13					
7	Grade Sch	9	9	22					
8	Total					GrnTot			
9									
10		Social Activity		(Expected)					
11	Education	AboveAvg	Average	BelowAvg	Total				
12	College								
13	High Sch								
14	Grade Sch								
15	Total								
16									
17		Social Activity		(Chi-Square Computations)					
18	Education	AboveAvg	Average	BelowAvg	Total				
19	College								
20	High Sch								
21	Grade Sch								
22	Total								
23									
24	df								
25	Alpha								
26	Crit_Val								
27	Conclusion								
28									

10. In cell B26, key =**CHIINV(Alpha,df)**

11. In cell B27, key =**IF(Chi_Sq>Crit_Val, "Reject Ho", "Do Not Reject Ho")**

12. Highlight **A24:B26**. From the Menu bar select Insert. Select Name. Select Create. Select Left Column. Click on OK. If you are asked if you would like to replace the existing definition, click on Yes.

13. Highlight **B5:B7**. From the Tool bar select the AutoSum button.

14. Make B8 your active cell. To copy, drag the lower right handle to cells C8:D8.

15. Highlight **B5:D5**. From the Tool bar select the AutoSum button.

16. Copy E5 into E6:E8.

17. Highlight **E8:F8**. Use the Name-Create function to name the cell. Use the Right Column.

The completed, summed, Observed table should look as shown below.

	A	B	C	D	E	F	G	H	I
1	Chi-Square Contingency Tables								
2									
3		Social Activity		(Observed)					
4	Education	AboveAvg	Average	BelowAvg	Total				
5	College	18	12	10	40				
6	High Sch	17	15	13	45				
7	Grade Sch	9	9	22	40				
8	Total	44	36	45	125	GrnTot			
9									

You will now compute the expected frequencies. For each cell the formula is
Expected frequency =(Row total)(Column total)/Grand total.

    18. In cell B12, key **=$E5*B$8/GrnTot**

This formula multiplies the row total (E5) times the column total (B8) and divides by the Grand Total which we named GrnTot. The $ sign in the formula keeps the appropriate row or column constant when it is copied into another cell.

    19. Make B12 your active cell. Copy the contents to B13:B14

    20. Highlight **B12:B14**. Drag the right handle of B14 to C14:D14.

    21. Sum the contents of B12:B14. Copy B15 to C15:D15.

    22. Sum the contents of B12:D12. Copy E12 to E13:E15.

The completed Expected table should look as shown below.

	A	B	C	D	E	F	G	H	I
10		Social Activity		(Expected)					
11	Education	AboveAvg	Average	BelowAvg	Total				
12	College	14.08	11.52	14.4	40				
13	High Sch	15.84	12.96	16.2	45				
14	Grade Sch	14.08	11.52	14.4	40				
15	Total	44	36	45	125				
16									

    23. In Cell B19, key =**(B5-B12)^2/B12**

This formula subtracts the expected value from the observed value, squares the difference and divides by the expected value. The formula for chi-square is the sum of all the computed results.

24. Copy B19 to B20:B21.

25. Highlight **B19:B21**. Drag the right handle of B21 to C21:D21.

26. In E22, key =**SUM(B19:D21)**

27. In F22, key **Chi_Sq**

28. Highlight **E22:F22**. Use the Name-Create function to name the cell. Use the Right Column.

The completed Chi-Square Computation table should look as shown below.

	A	B	C	D	E	F	G	H	I
17		Social Activity		(Chi-Square Computations)					
18	Education	AboveAvg	Average	BelowAvg	Total				
19	College	1.091364	0.02	1.344444					
20	High Sch	0.084949	0.321111	0.632099					
21	Grade Sch	1.832841	0.55125	4.011111					
22	Total				9.889169	Chi_Sq			
23									

The last thing you will do is enter the values for degrees of freedom and Alpha. The degrees of freedom is df = (number of rows - 1)(number of columns - 1). Or (3-1)(3-1) = 4.

29. In B24, key **4**

30. In B25, key **.05**

This completes your total worksheet and gives the resulting output.

	A	B	C	D	E	F	G	H	I
1	Chi-Square Contingency Tables								
2									
3		Social Activity		(Observed)					
4	Education	AboveAvg	Average	BelowAvg	Total				
5	College	18	12	10	40				
6	High Sch	17	15	13	45				
7	Grade Sch	9	9	22	40				
8	Total	44	36	45	125	GrnTot			
9									
10		Social Activity		(Expected)					
11	Education	AboveAvg	Average	BelowAvg	Total				
12	College	14.08	11.52	14.4	40				
13	High Sch	15.84	12.96	16.2	45				
14	Grade Sch	14.08	11.52	14.4	40				
15	Total	44	36	45	125				
16									
17		Social Activity		(Chi-Square Computations)					
18	Education	AboveAvg	Average	BelowAvg	Total				
19	College	1.091364	0.02	1.344444					
20	High Sch	0.084949	0.321111	0.632099					
21	Grade Sch	1.832841	0.55125	4.011111					
22	Total				9.889169	Chi_Sq			
23									
24	df	4							
25	Alpha	0.05							
26	Crit_Val	9.487728							
27	Conclusion	Reject Ho							
28									

The results can now be interpreted.

The null hypothesis is rejected at the .05 level of significance. The computed value for chi-square, 9.889169 is greater than the critical value of 9.487728. There is a relationship between the level of education and the frequency of social activity. People with a college education have a higher level of social activity.

Save your file as **chi-sqcn**. Close your file.

Example 4. To use this worksheet to solve problems having other than 3 rows and 3 columns, you must modify the worksheet. If you insert rows and columns, (or delete rows and columns) **between** existing rows and columns, you will not have to re-compute the existing row and column sums. They will adjust automatically. If you insert rows or columns you will need to copy existing formulas to the inserted cells. You will also need to enter the new value for the degrees of freedom.

In example 3, assume the sociologist wanted four levels of education in her study. She also researched graduate school students. Her data for graduate school students was 10 above average, 6 average and 4 below average.

1. Open the file **chi-sqcn**.

2. Make A6 your active cell. From the Menu bar select Insert. Select Rows.

This inserts a blank row between two existing categories. As you key in the extra data you will notice that the totals in row 9 and column E will automatically change to reflect the current data.

3. In cell A5, key **Grad Sch**.

4. In cell A6, key **College**.

5. Make A14 your active cell. Insert a row.

6. Make A22 your active cell. Insert a row.

7. In cells A13 and A21, key **Grad Sch**.

8. In cells A14 and A22, key **College**.

9. In cells B6:D6, key **18**, **12**, and **10** respectively.

10. In cells B5:D5, key **10**, **7**, and **3**, respectively.

After these changes, your worksheet should look as shown on the next page.

	A	B	C	D	E	F	G	H	I
1	Chi-Square Contingency Tables								
2									
3		Social Activity		(Observed)					
4	Education	AboveAvg	Average	BelowAvg	Total				
5	Grad Sch	10	7	3	20				
6	College	18	12	10					
7	High Sch	17	15	13	45				
8	Grade Sch	9	9	22	40				
9	Total	54	43	48	145	GrnTot			
10									
11		Social Activity		(Expected)					
12	Education	AboveAvg	Average	BelowAvg	Total				
13	Grad Sch	7.448276	5.931034	6.62069	20				
14	College								
15	High Sch	16.75862	13.34483	14.89655	45				
16	Grade Sch	14.89655	11.86207	13.24138	40				
17	Total	39.10345	31.13793	34.75862	105				
18									
19		Social Activity		(Chi-Square Computations)					
20	Education	AboveAvg	Average	BelowAvg	Total				
21	Grad Sch	0.874202	0.192662	1.980065					
22	College								
23	High Sch	0.003477	0.205293	0.241459					
24	Grade Sch	2.334052	0.690557	5.793463					
25	Total				12.31523	Chi_Sq			
26									
27	df	4							
28	Alpha	0.05							
29	Crit_Val	9.487728							
30	Conclusior	Reject Ho							
31									

You now need to copy the formulas to the blank cells

    11. Copy E5 to E6.

    12. Highlight **B13:E13**. Drag the right handle of E13 to E14.

    13. Highlight **B21:D21**. Drag the right handle of D21 to D22.

The only thing left to do is to put in a new value for the degrees of freedom. Since there are now 4 rows and 3 columns, the degrees of freedom is $(4-1)(3-1) = 6$.

    14. In B27, key **6**.

The output in the worksheet has changed to reflect the changed data.

	A	B	C	D	E	F	G	H	I
1	Chi-Square Contingency Tables								
2									
3		Social Activity		(Observed)					
4	Education	AboveAvg	Average	BelowAvg	Total				
5	Grad Sch	10	7	3	20				
6	College	18	12	10	40				
7	High Sch	17	15	13	45				
8	Grade Sch	9	9	22	40				
9	Total	54	43	48	145	GrnTot			
10									
11		Social Activity		(Expected)					
12	Education	AboveAvg	Average	BelowAvg	Total				
13	Grad Sch	7.448276	5.931034	6.62069	20				
14	College	14.89655	11.86207	13.24138	40				
15	High Sch	16.75862	13.34483	14.89655	45				
16	Grade Sch	14.89655	11.86207	13.24138	40				
17	Total	54	43	48	145				
18									
19		Social Activity		(Chi-Square Computations)					
20	Education	AboveAvg	Average	BelowAvg	Total				
21	Grad Sch	0.874202	0.192662	1.980065					
22	College	0.646552	0.001604	0.793463					
23	High Sch	0.003477	0.205293	0.241459					
24	Grade Sch	2.334052	0.690557	5.793463					
25	Total				13.75685	Chi_Sq			
26									
27	df	6							
28	Alpha	0.05							
29	Crit_Val	12.59158							
30	Conclusion	Reject Ho							
31									

If you wish, save your file as **chi-sq4**. Close your file.

Practice Exercises taken from textbook.

In addition to showing your printout, state the results of the hypothesis test in terms of the question using complete sentences and examples.

15-1. A group of department store buyers viewed a new line of dresses and gave their opinions of them. The results were: (Textbook Problem 15-7)

Opinion	Frequency
Outstanding	47
Excellent	45
Very good	40
Good	39
Fair	35
Undesirable	34

Because the largest number (47) indicated the new line is outstanding, the head designer thinks that this is a mandate to go into mass production of the dresses. The head sweeper (who somehow became involved in this) believes that there is not a clear mandate and claims that the opinions are evenly distributed among the six categories. He further says that the slight differences among the various counts are probably due to chance. Test the null hypothesis that there is no significant difference among the opinions of the buyers. Test at the .01 level of risk. Follow a formal approach, that is, state the null hypothesis, the alternate hypothesis, and so on.

15-2. The safety director of Honda USA took samples at random from the file of motor accidents and classified them according to the time the time the accident took place. (Textbook Problem 15-8)

Time	Number of accidents	Time	Number of accidents
8 up to 9 A.M.	6	1 up to 2 P.M.	7
9 up to 10 A.M.	6	2 up to 3 P.M.	8
10 up to 11 A.M.	20	3 up to 4 P.M.	19
11 up to 12 P.M.	8	4 up to 5 P.M.	6

Using the goodness of fit test and the .01 level of significance, determine whether or not the accidents are evenly distributed throughout the day.

15-3. A study regarding the relationship between age and the amount of pressure sales personnel feel in relation to their jobs revealed the following sample information. At the .01 significance level, is there a relationship between job pressure and age? (Textbook Problem 15-26)

	Degree of job pressure		
Age (years)	Low	Medium	High
Less than 25	20	18	22
25 up to 40	50	46	44
40 up to 60	58	63	59
60 and older	34	43	43

15-4. A sample of employees at a large chemical plant was asked to indicate a preference for one of three pension plans. The results are given in the following table. Does it seem that there is a relationship between the pension plan selected and the job classification of the employee? Use the .01 significance level. (Textbook Problem 15-28)

	Pension Plan		
Job class	Plan A	Plan B	Plan C
Supervisor	10	13	29
Clerical	19	80	19
Labor	81	57	22

CHAPTER
16
NONPARAMETRIC METHODS: ANALYSIS OF RANKED DATA

CHAPTER GOALS

After completing this chapter, you will be able to:

1. Create and use a template to perform the sign test for dependent samples using the normal approximation to the binomial.

2. Create a template for solving problems using the Wilcoxon Rank-Sum Test.

Introduction

Chapter 16 is a continuation of tests of hypotheses designed for nonparametric or distribution–free data. The chi-square applications in Chapter 15 required only nominal-level data whereas the tests in this chapter require data that is at least ordinal level, that is, data that can be ranked from low to high. We will show how Excel can be used for the **sign test** and the **Wilcoxon rank-sum test**. As with the chi-square distribution, the nonparametric distributions in this chapter are also positively skewed.

You will continue to use the 5 steps in hypothesis testing:
1. **State the null and alternative hypothesis** using either formulas or words. The null hypothesis (H_o) is always the statement of no significant difference. The alternative hypothesis (H_1) is always the statement that there is a significant difference. When direction is stated it is a one-directional test (one-tailed). When direction is not stated it is a two-directional test (two-tailed).

2. **State the level of significance** or the probability that the null hypothesis is rejected when, in fact, it is true.

3. **State the statistical test** you will be using: the z-test, t-test, f-test, chi square test, etc.

4. **Formulate a decision rule**. Using a picture or curve that estimates the distribution you are testing, show the critical value if you are performing a one-directional test or the upper and lower critical values if you are performing a two-directional test.

5. **Do it**. Show the formula you used and at least the major steps involved. State the results of the hypothesis test in terms of the question using complete sentences and examples.

The Sign Test

The **sign test** is based on the sign, usually plus "+" or minus "-", of a difference between two related observations. With the sign test, we are not concerned with the magnitude of the difference, only the direction of the difference. A popular use of the sign test is to check the results of an experiment, for example, recording the performance of employees before and after a training exercise. If the training was not effective or had no impact on performance about half the employees trained would show improved performance and about half would show a decrease in performance. Another use of the sign test is product-preference.

Example 1: Creating a template for solving problems using the sign test, where the sample is larger than 10.

The formula for finding the z-value in the sign test is $z = \dfrac{(X \pm .50) - \mu}{\sigma}$ where,

$$\mu = .50n$$
$$\sigma = .50\sqrt{n}$$

So the formula becomes $z = \dfrac{(X \pm .50) - .50n}{.50\sqrt{n}}$

X is the number of positive or negative outcomes in the sample size. It is referred to as X.

n is the sample size. It will be referred to as n.

1. Retrieve the file **1sa-mean**

2. In A1, key **Test of Hypotheses**

3. In A2, key **Sign Test**

You need to delete the rows containing the cell names so you can create new names.

4. Highlight A5:A6. From the Menu bar select <u>E</u>dit. Select <u>D</u>elete. Select radio button for Entire <u>r</u>ow. Select OK.

5. Highlight A6. From the Menu bar select <u>E</u>dit. Select <u>D</u>elete. Select radio button for Entire <u>r</u>ow. Select OK.

6. Immediately from the Menu bar select <u>I</u>nsert. Select <u>R</u>ows.

7. In cell A6, key **X.**

8. Highlight A6:B6. From the Menu bar, select <u>I</u>nsert. Select <u>N</u>ame. Select <u>C</u>reate. Select the check box for <u>L</u>eft Column. Select OK

9. In B9, key **=IF(X<n/2,(X+0.5-0.5*n)/(0.5*SQRT(n)),(X-0.5-0.5*n)/(0.5*SQRT(n)))**

This computes the z-value for this test.

Some cells will read #DIV?0! or #NUM!. They will be filled in as you find the values for the variables.

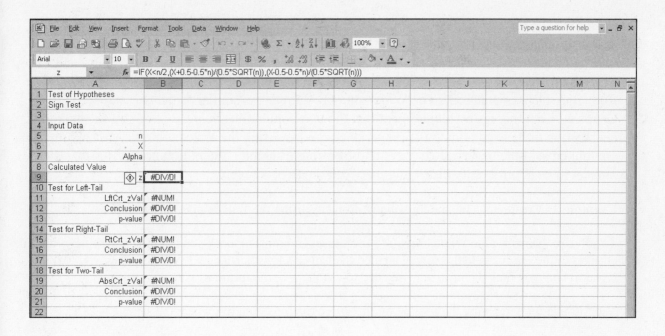

Save your file as **sign test**

Example 2: The market research department of Cola, Inc has been given the assignment of testing a new soft drink. Two versions of the drink are considered – a rather sweet drink and a somewhat bitter one. A preference test is conducted consisting of a sampling of 64 consumers. Each consumer tasted both the sweet cola and the bitter one and indicated a preference. Out of the 64 sampled, 42 preferred the sweet cola. At the .05 significance level is there a preference between the two colas?

1. Open the file **sign test** if it is not already open.

2. In cell B5, key **64**, the sample number.

3. In cell B6, key **42**

4. In cell B7 key, **.05**, alpha for this problem.

Bold cells B9 and B20.

This completes the problem.

Since the z value of 2.38 (rounded) is greater than the absolute critical z-value of 1.96 (rounded), reject the null hypothesis. There is evidence of a difference in consumer preference.

If you wish, save your file as **Ch16-prob1**

	A	B	C
1	Test of Hypotheses		
2	Sign Test		
3			
4	Input Data		
5	n	64	
6	X	42	
7	Alpha	0.05	
8	Calculated Value		
9	z	2.375	
10	Test for Left-Tail		
11	LftCrt_zVal	-1.64485	
12	Conclusion	Do Not Reject Ho	
13	p-value	0.991226	
14	Test for Right-Tail		
15	RtCrt_zVal	1.644853	
16	Conclusion	Reject Ho	
17	p-value	0.008774	
18	Test for Two-Tail		
19	AbsCrt_zVal	1.959963	
20	Conclusion	**Reject Ho**	
21	p-value	0.017549	
22			

The Wilcoxon Rank-Sum Test

The **Wilcoxon rank-sum test** is designed to determine whether two independent samples came from equivalent populations. The Wilcoxon rank-sum test is similar to the two-sample t test in Chapter 11 but there is no requirement that the two populations being studied follow the normal distribution or have equal population variances. When using the Wilcoxon rank-sum test the data are ranked as if the observations were part of a single sample. The null hypothesis is that the ranks will be about evenly distributed between the two samples.

Example 3: Creating a template for solving problems using the Wilcoxon Rank-Sum Test.

To solve problems for the Wilcoxon rank-sum test several things must be done. First you will make some changes to the 1sa-mean template you created in chapter 8 to create a new template. Then you will use Excel to help you rank the raw data you need to use to solve the formula.

The formula for computing the z-value for the Wilcoxon rank-sum test where the sample is at least 8 is:

$$z = \frac{W - \frac{n_1(n_1 + n_2 + 1)}{2}}{\sqrt{\frac{n_1 n_2 (n_1 + n_2 + 1)}{12}}}$$

W is the sum of the ranks from the first population, it will be referred to as W.
n_1 is the number of observations from the first population, it will be referred to as n_1.
n_2 is the number of observations from the second population, it will be referred to as n_2.

1. Retrieve the file **1samean**

2. In A1, key **Test of Hypotheses**

3. In A2, key **Wilcoxon Rank-Sum Test**

You need to delete the rows containing the cell names so you can create new names.

4. Highlight A5:A8. From the Menu bar select Edit. Select Delete. Select radio button for Entire row. Select OK.

5. Highlight A5:A7. From the Menu bar select Insert. Select Rows. From the tool bar click on Align Right icon.

6. Highlight A10. From the Menu bar select Edit. Select Delete. Select radio button for Entire row. Select OK.

	A	B	C
1	Test of Hypotheses		
2	Wilcoxon Rank-Sum Test		
3			
4	Input Data		
5	n_1		
6	n_2		
7	W		
8	Alpha		
9	Calculated Value		
10	z	#DIV/0!	
11	Test for Left-Tail		
12	LftCrt_zVal	#NUM!	
13	Conclusion	#DIV/0!	
14	p-value	#DIV/0!	
15	Test for Right-Tail		
16	RtCrt_zVal	#NUM!	
17	Conclusion	#DIV/0!	
18	p-value	#DIV/0!	
19	Test for Two-Tail		
20	AbsCrt_zVal	#NUM!	
21	Conclusion	#DIV/0!	
22	p-value	#DIV/0!	
23			

7. Immediately from the Menu bar select Insert. Select Rows. From the tool bar click on Align Right icon.

8. In A5:A7, key **n_1**, **n_2**, and **W** respectively.

9. In A10, key **z**

10. In B10, key **=(W-(n_1*(n_1+n_2+1)/2))/SQRT((n_1*n_2*(n_1+n_2+1)/12))**

Cell B10 will read #NAME?

11. Highlight A5:B7. From the Menu bar, select Insert. Select Name. Select Create. Select the check box for Left Column. Click on OK.

12. Highlight A10:B10. From the Menu bar, select Insert. Select Name. Select Create. Select the check box for Left Column. Click OK. If you are asked if you want to replace existing definition of 'z', click Yes.

Some cells will read #DIV/0! or #NUM!. They will be filled in as you find the values for the variables.

The cell contents of A5-B12 will look as follows.

	A	B	C	D	E	F	G
4							
5	n_1						
6	n_2						
7	W						
8	Alpha						
9	Calculated Value						
10	z	=(W-(n_1*(n_1+n_2+1)/2))/SQRT((n_1*n_2*(n_1+n_2+1)/12))					
11							

Save your file as **wilcox-rank**

Example 4: Dan Thompson, the president of CEO Airlines, recently noted an increase in the number of no-shows for flights out of Atlanta. He is particularly interested in determining whether there are more no-shows for flights that originate from Atlanta compared with flights leaving Chicago. A sample of nine flights from Atlanta and eight from Chicago are listed below. At the .05 significance level, can we conclude that there are more no-shows for the flights originating in Atlanta?

Atlanta	11	15	10	18	11	20	24	22	25
Chicago	13	14	10	8	16	9	17	21	

Using Excel to rank data
Now you will use Excel to help rank the data so you can complete the problem.

1. Open the file **wilcox-rank**, if it is not already open.

2. At the bottom of your same worksheet, click on the Sheet 2 tab. This will give you a clean sheet to rank your data.

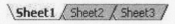

3. In cell **A1**, key **A** (for Atlanta). In cell **A10**, key **C** (for Chicago).

4. To drag the contents in **A1** to **A2:A9**, make **A1** your active cell. Put your mouse pointer on the lower right corner of the cell. It will show a small black box called a handle. The mouse pointer on the handle will show as a thick, black plus. Click your mouse button, hold and drag the mouse pointer down to cell **A9**.

5. Drag the contents in **A10** to **A11:A17**.

6. In **B1:B9**, enter the data for Atlanta.

7. In **B10:B17**, enter the data for Chicago.

	A	B	C
1	A	10	
2	A	11	
3	A	11	
4	A	15	
5	A	18	
6	A	20	
7	A	22	
8	A	24	
9	A	25	
10	C	8	
11	C	9	
12	C	10	
13	C	13	
14	C	14	
15	C	16	
16	C	17	
17	C	21	
18			

Your worksheet will look as shown.

8. Place your cursor anywhere in column B. From the Tool bar, click on the Sort Ascending icon.

This arranges all the data in order so you can rank it.

9. In column C, place the rank of each value as discussed in the textbook.

10. Place your cursor anywhere in column A. From the Tool bar, click on the Sort Ascending icon.

	A	B	C	D
1	C	8	1	
2	C	9	2	
3	A	10	3.5	
4	C	10	3.5	
5	A	11	5.5	
6	A	11	5.5	
7	C	13	7	
8	C	14	8	
9	A	15	9	
10	C	16	10	
11	C	17	11	
12	A	18	12	
13	A	20	13	
14	C	21	14	
15	A	22	15	
16	A	24	16	
17	A	25	17	
18				

This arranges the data back into being grouped by Atlanta and Chicago. Since Atlanta is the first population, you want the sum of the ranks for Atlanta.

11. In cell D9 key **=SUM(C1:C9)**

This gives you the sum of the ranks for Atlanta and gives you the value of W that you need to compute the z value.

	A	B	C	D	E	F	G	H	I
1	A	10	3.5						
2	A	11	5.5						
3	A	11	5.5						
4	A	15	9						
5	A	18	12						
6	A	20	13						
7	A	22	15						
8	A	24	16						
9	A	25	17	96.5					
10	C	8	1						
11	C	9	2						
12	C	10	3.5						
13	C	13	7						
14	C	14	8						
15	C	16	10						
16	C	17	11						
17	C	21	14						
18									
19									
20									

Sum=96.5

12. At the bottom of your worksheet, click on the Sheet 1 tab.

13. In cell B5, key **9**, the number of observations from the first population.

14. In cell B6, key **8**, the number of observations from the second population.

15. In cell B7, key **96.5**, the sum of the ranks for Atlanta you just computed in sheet 2.

16. In cell B8, key **.05**, the alpha in this problem for finding the critical value.

Bold cells B10 and B17.

This completes the problem.

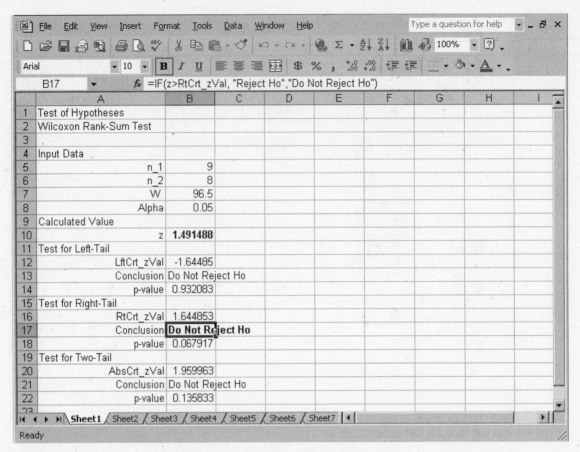

This is a right-tailed test. We do not reject the null hypothesis, since 1.49 (rounded) is less than 1.65 (rounded).

The evidence does not show a difference in the typical number of no-shows.

If you wish, save your file as **Ch16-prob2**

Practice Exercises taken from textbook

16-1.   A sample of 45 overweight men participated in an exercise program. At the conclusion of the program 32 had lost weight. At the .05 significance level, can we conclude the program is effective? (Textbook Problem 16-5)

16-2.   Pierre's Restaurant announced that on Thursday night the menu would consist of unusual gourmet items, such as squid, rabbit, snails from Scotland, and dandelion greens. As part of a larger survey, a sample of 81 regular customers was asked whether they preferred the regular menu or the gourmet menu. Forty-three preferred the gourmet menu. Using the sign test and the .02 significance level, test whether the customers liked the gourmet menu better than the regular menu. (Textbook Problem 16-7)

16-3.   The following observations were randomly selected from populations that were not necessarily normally distributed. Use the .05 significance level, a two-tailed test, and the Wilcoxon rank-sum test to determine whether there is a difference between the two populations. (Textbook Problem 16-15)

Population A:	38	45,	56	57	61	69	70	79
Population B:	26	31	35	42	51	52	57	62

16-4.   Tucson State University offers two MBA programs. In the first program the students meet two nights per week at the University's main campus in downtown Tucson. In the second program students only communicated on-line with the instructor. The director of the MBA experience at Tucson wishes to compare the number of hours studied last week by the two groups of students. A sample of 10 on-campus students and 12 on-line students revealed the following information. (Textbook Problem 16-17)

Campus	28	16	42	29	31	22	50	42	23	25		
Online	26	42	65	38	29	32	59	42	27	41	46	18

Do not assume the two distributions of study times, which are reported in hours, follow a normal distribution. At the .05 significance level, can we conclude the on-line students study more?

CHAPTER
17
STATISTICAL QUALITY CONTROL

CHAPTER GOALS

After completing this chapter, you will be able to:

1. Discuss the importance of statistical quality control.

2. Define several terms unique to quality control, including chance causes and assignable causes, in control and out of control.

3. Use Excel to construct two types of control charts: mean charts and percent defective charts.

Introduction

The objective of **statistical quality control** is to monitor production through the many stages of manufacturing and to monitor the quality of services. Quality control charts allow us to identify when a production process or a service becomes "out of control."

During the 1920s, the concepts of statistical quality control were developed, primarily through the work of Dr. Walter A. Shewhart of the Bell Telephone Laboratories. Shewhart introduced the concept of "controlling " quality during the production process rather than inspecting it into the part. He used control charts to help with this process. He also introduced the concept of statistical sampling inspections to estimate whether manufactured lots were good or bad, replacing the old method of inspecting every part.

W. Edwards Deming expanded on Shewhart's work by emphasizing that quality originates from improving the process, not from "inspecting out" the unsatisfactory results of poor production. The Fourteen Points of the Deming Management Method and the Seven Deadly Diseases of the Deming Management Method helped many companies in Japan and the United States improve product quality and reduce cost by using statistical quality control techniques.

There are two general causes of variation in manufacturing process: **chance and assignable variation.** Chance variations are usually large in number and random in nature, and they cannot be eliminated without changing the process. Assignable variation is usually non-random in nature and can be eliminated or reduced. It is often possible to fix what is causing the variation.

When a process is being monitored by a control chart and all of the observations fall within the upper and lower control limits, we are observing chance variation and the process is **in control**. When the process observations fall outside the upper and lower control limits, we are observing assignable variation and the process is **out of control.**

The following examples show how you can use Excel to aid in statistical quality control by constructing control charts.

Mean Charts

You will be using Excel's ChartWizard to plot the means and create a mean chart which portrays the fluctuation in the sample means.

Example 1. Every hour the quality-control inspector checks four pieces and records the outside diameters of each of the four pieces. The results are shown in the following table.

Time	Sample piece			
	1	2	3	4
9 am	1	4	5	2
10 am	2	3	2	1
11 am	1	7	3	5

Plot the sample means. Compute the overall mean, determine the control limits, and show the limits and the mean on a mean chart.

1. On a new worksheet enter the data as shown below.

We place the Mean column next to the Time column to make it easier when we create the chart.

2. In B3, key =**AVERAGE(C3:F3)**

3. Place your mouse arrow on the lower right handle of B3. It will look like a thick black plus sign. Click and drag to B4:B5.

4. Highlight **A3:B5**. From the Tool bar select ChartWizard.

5. In Step 1, under Chart type, select line. Under Chart sub-type, select the left chart in the middle row. Click Next.

6. In Step 2, accept the defaults. Click Next.

7. In Step 3, at the top, the Titles tab should be selected. Click on the Chart title text box, key **Mean Chart for Diameters**. Tab to the Category (X) axis text box. Leave this text box blank so the chart will appear larger. Tab to the Value (Y) axis text box. Key **Diameter**.

8. At the top, select the Legend tab. Click in the Show legend check box to de-select the legend.

9. At the top select Gridlines. Under Value (Y) axis, click in the Major gridline text box to deselect the gridline. Click Finish.

A condensed chart appears.

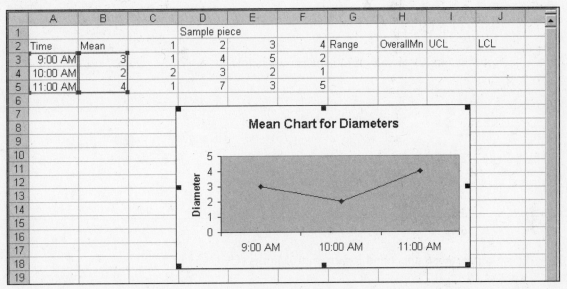

10. With the handles still on the chart, click and hold the left mouse button inside the chart. A 4-way arrow will show in the chart. As you move the chart it will show as an open box with dashed lines. With your mouse button still depressed, drag your mouse and move your chart so the left edge of the chart is in column K and the top edge of the chart is in row 1.

11. Click on the bottom handle of the chart. Drag the bottom line to row 17.

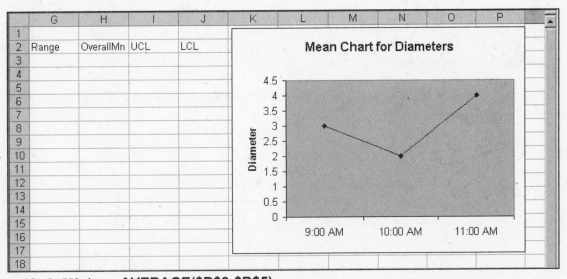

12. In H3, key =AVERAGE($B$3:$B$5)

This computes the mean of the sample means. The $ sign in the formula keeps the formula from changing when you copy it into other cells.

13. Copy H3 to H4:H5.

14. In G3, key =**MAX(C3:F3)-MIN(C3:F3)**

This computes the sample range (difference) of the data.

15. Copy G3 to G4:G5.

At this point your data in A1:J5 should look as shown below.

	A	B	C	D	E	F	G	H	I	J
1				Sample piece						
2	Time	Mean	1	2	3	4	Range	OverallMn	UCL	LCL
3	9am	3	1	4	5	2	4	3		
4	10am	2	2	3	2	1	2	3		
5	11am	4	1	7	3	5	6	3		
6										

You will now compute the upper and lower control limits (UCL and LCL).

The formulas are UCL = $\overline{\overline{X}} + A_2\overline{R}$, and LCL = $\overline{\overline{X}} - A_2\overline{R}$

$\overline{\overline{X}}$ 1 is the mean of the sample means (the Overall Mean that was computed in instruction 12.)

$\overline{R}$ 2 is the mean of the sample ranges.

16. In F6, key **RangeMn**.

17. In G6, key =**AVERAGE(G3:G5)**

This computes the mean of the sample ranges.

A_2 is a factor obtained from APPENDIX B of your text book titled FACTORS FOR CONTROL CHARTS.

A partial table is shown below. To find the factor, first locate the sample size, n (4 in this example) in the left margin. Then move horizontally to the A_2 column and read the factor. It is .729.

Factors for control charts
Chart of averages

Number of items in sample	Factors for control limits
n	A_2
2	1.880
3	1.023
4	.729
5	.577
6	.483

You now have all the information needed to compute the upper and lower limits.

18. In I3, key =**H3+.729*$G$6**

19. In J3, key =**H3-.729*$G$6**

20. Highlight **I3:J3**. Drag the lower right handle of J3 to J4:J5.

At this point your data in A1:J6 should look as shown below.

	A	B	C	D	E	F	G	H	I	J
1				Sample piece						
2	Time	Mean	1	2	3	4	Range	OverallMn	UCL	LCL
3	9am	3	1	4	5	2	4	3	5.916	0.084
4	10am	2	2	3	2	1	2	3	5.916	0.084
5	11am	4	1	7	3	5	6	3	5.916	0.084
6						RangeMn	4			
7										

Click on the bottom scroll bar so you can see columns H through P on your screen.

You will now add the Overall Mean and upper and lower limits to the existing chart.

21. Highlight **H3:J5**. Place your mouse arrow on one of the outside lines. Make sure your mouse arrow remains an arrow.

22. Click and drag the box on top of the chart. As you move your mouse arrow, an open shadow box is displayed. Place the shadow box into the chart. It will change to a small plus (+) sign.

The chart now shows the Overall Mean and upper and lower limits as well as the means of the samples.

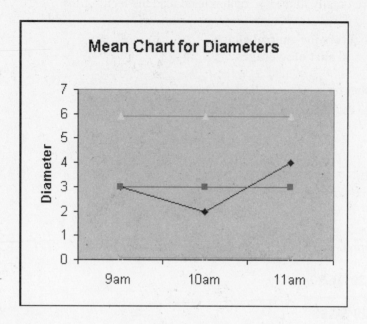

You will now modify the chart to make it more meaningful.

23. Click on the chart so the handles are around it.

24. Click your **right** mouse arrow on the vertical Y-axis. Choose Format Axis. In the Format Axis dialog box, select the Scale tab. In the Minimum text box key –1. In the Maximum text box key 7. The check boxes for Minimum and Maximum will not be selected. Click OK.

25. Click your **right** mouse arrow on the horizontal X-axis. Choose Format Axis. Choose the Scale tab. Click the check box for Value (Y) Axis crosses between categories, to deselect this option. Click OK.

26. **Right** click on the upper control limit line. Choose Format Data Series. In the Format Data Series text box, select the Patterns tab. In the Line column select Automatic. In the Marker column select None. Click OK.

Click anywhere off the line and the marker points for the upper control limit line are gone.

27. Repeat step 26 to remove the markers for the Overall Mean line and the lower control limit line.

Your chart now looks as shown.

The last procedure is to identify the lines.

28. With the chart still activated, key **OAM**. Touch the <Enter> key.

The label OAM, (which stands for Overall mean) shows in the middle of the chart with a shadow box around it.

29. Place your mouse arrow on the top line of the shadow box *between* two handles. The arrow will remain an arrow with a 4-way directional arrow just above it. Click and drag the shadow box until it is beside the middle line.

30. Repeat the directions in instructions 28 and 29 to place the label **UCL**, next to the top line and the label **LCL** next to the bottom line.

Click anywhere outside the chart. Your chart should appear as shown below.

If you wish, save your file as **mn-cht1**. Close your file.

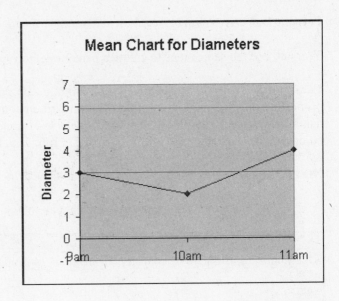

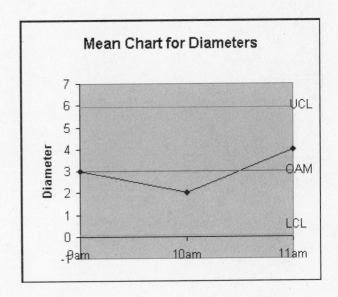

Percent Defective Chart

You will use the same steps to create a percent defective chart.

Example 2. The Inter State Moving and Storage Company is setting up a control chart to monitor the proportion of residential moves that result in written complaints due to late delivery, lost items, or damaged items. A sample of 50 moves is selected for each of the last 12 months. The number of written complaints in each sample is: 8, 7, 4, 8, 2, 7, 11, 6, 7, 6, 8, 12.

NOTE: You are using each "written complaint" as a "defective move".

1. On a new worksheet, enter the data as shown below.

	A	B	C	D	E	F	G	H	I
1	Month	NumSel	NumCmpl	ProDef	MnProDef	ULC	LCL		
2	Jan	50	8						
3	Feb	50	7						
4	Mar	50	4						
5	Apr	50	8						
6	May	50	2						
7	Jun	50	7						
8	Jul	50	11						
9	Aug	50	6						
10	Sep	50	7						
11	Oct	50	6						
12	Nov	50	8						
13	Dec	50	12						
14									

2. In D2, key =**C2/B2**

This gives the proportion defective.

3. Copy D2 to D3:D13.

4. Highlight **D2:D13**. From the Menu bar, select ChartWizard.

5. In Step 1, under Chart type, select line. Under Chart sub-type, select the left chart in the middle row. Click Next.

6. In Step 2, accept the defaults. Click Next.

7. In Step 3, at the top, the Titles tab should be selected. Click on the Chart title text box, key **Percent Defective Chart**. Tab to the Category (X) axis text box, key **Month** . Tab to the Value (Y) axis text box. Key **Proportion Defective**.

8. At the top, select the Legend tab. Click in the Show legend check box to de-select the legend.

9. At the top, select Gridlines. Under Value (Y) axis, click in the Major gridline text box to deselect the gridline. Click Finish.

A condensed chart appears.

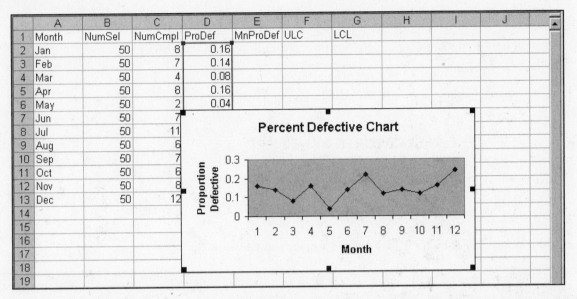

10. With the handles still on the chart, click and hold the left mouse button inside the chart. A 4-way arrow will show in the chart. As you move the chart it will show as an open box with dashed lines. With your mouse button still depressed, drag your mouse and move your chart so the left edge of the chart is in column H and the top edge of the chart is in row 1.

11. Click on the bottom handle of the chart. Drag the bottom line to row 17.

12. Highlight **D2:D13**. From the Menu bar, select AutoSum.

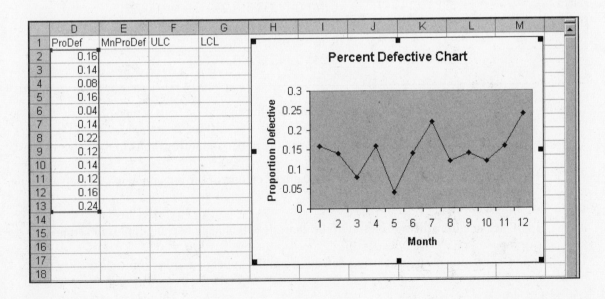

13. In E2, key **=$D$14/12**

This computes $\bar{p}$ (the mean proportion defective).

14. Copy E2 to E3:E13.

You will now compute the upper and lower control limits (UCL and LCL).

The formulas are UCL = $\bar{p}$ + $3\sqrt{\dfrac{p(1-p)}{n}}$, and LCL = $\bar{p}$ - $3\sqrt{\dfrac{p(1-p)}{n}}$.

15. In F2, key **=E2+3*SQRT(E2*(1-E2)/B2)**

16. In G2, key **=E2-3*SQRT(E2*(1-E2)/B2)**

17. Highlight **F2:G2**. Drag the lower right handle of G2 to G3:G13.

At this point your data in A1:G14 should look as shown below.

	A	B	C	D	E	F	G	H	I
1	Month	NumSel	NumCmpl	ProDef	MnProDef	ULC	LCL		
2	Jan	50	8	0.16	0.143333	0.292001	-0.00533		
3	Feb	50	7	0.14	0.143333	0.292001	-0.00533		
4	Mar	50	4	0.08	0.143333	0.292001	-0.00533		
5	Apr	50	8	0.16	0.143333	0.292001	-0.00533		
6	May	50	2	0.04	0.143333	0.292001	-0.00533		
7	Jun	50	7	0.14	0.143333	0.292001	-0.00533		
8	Jul	50	11	0.22	0.143333	0.292001	-0.00533		
9	Aug	50	6	0.12	0.143333	0.292001	-0.00533		
10	Sep	50	7	0.14	0.143333	0.292001	-0.00533		
11	Oct	50	6	0.12	0.143333	0.292001	-0.00533		
12	Nov	50	8	0.16	0.143333	0.292001	-0.00533		
13	Dec	50	12	0.24	0.143333	0.292001	-0.00533		
14				1.72					

Click on the bottom scroll bar so you can see columns E through M on your screen.

You will now add the mean proportion defective, and the upper and lower limits to the existing chart.

18. Highlight E2:G13. Place your mouse arrow on one of the outside lines. Make sure your mouse arrow remains an arrow.

19. Click and drag the box on top of the chart. It will change to a small plus (+) sign.

The chart now shows the mean proportion defective and the upper and lower limits as well as the proportion defective.

You will now modify the chart to make it more meaningful.

20. Click on the chart so the handles are around it.

21. Click your **right** mouse arrow on the horizontal X-axis. Choose F̲ormat Axis. Choose the Scale tab. Click the check box for Value (Y) Axis crosses b̲etween categories, to deselect this option. Click OK.

22. **Right** click on the upper control limit line. Choose F̲ormat Data Series. In the Format Data Series text box, select the Pattern tab. In the Line column select Automatic. In the Marker column select N̲one. Click OK.

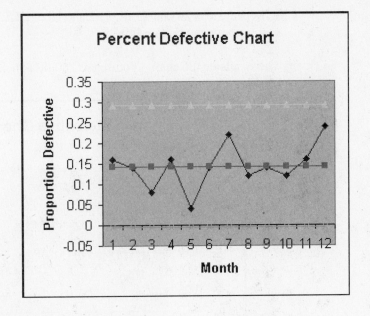

Click anywhere off the line and the marker points for the upper control limit line are gone.

23. Repeat the directions in instruction 22 to remove the markers for the mean proportion defective line and the lower control limit line.

Your chart now looks as shown.

The last procedure is to identify the lines.

24. With the chart still activated, key **MPD**. Touch the <Enter> key.

The label MPD, (which stands for Mean Proportion Defective) shows in the middle of the chart with a shadow box around it.

25. Place your mouse arrow on the top line of the shadow box *between* two handles. The arrow will remain an arrow with a 4-way directional arrow just above it. Click and drag the shadow box until it is beside the middle line.

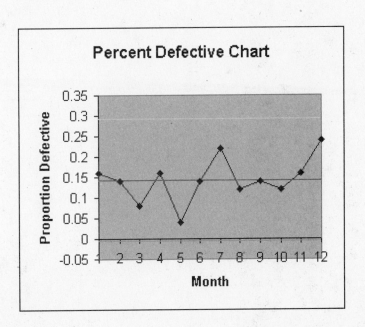

26. Repeat steps 24 and 25 to place the label **UCL**, just below the top line and the label **LCL** just above the bottom line.

Click anywhere outside the chart. Your chart should appear as shown below.

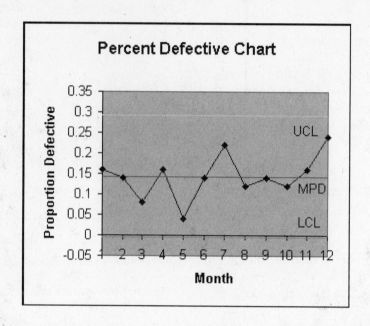

If you wish, save your file as **pro-cht1**. Close your file.

Practice Exercise taken from textbook.

17-1. A new machine has just been installed to cut and rough-shape large slugs. The slugs are then transferred to a precision grinder. One critical measurement is the outside diameter. The quality-control inspector was instructed to select five slugs at random every half hour from the output of the new machine, measure the outside diameter, and record the results. The measurements (in millimeters) for the period from 8:00 a.m. to 10:30 a.m. follow. (Textbook Problem 17-20)

Time	**Outside diameter (millimeters)**				
	1	2	3	4	5
8:00	87.1	87.3	87.9	87.0	87.0
8:30	86.9	88.5	87.6	87.5	87.4
9:00	87.5	88.4	86.9	87.6	88.2
9:30	86.0	88.0	87.2	87.6	87.1
10:00	87.1	87.1	87.1	87.1	87.1
10:30	88.0	86.2	87.4	87.3	87.8

a. Design a mean chart. Insert the control limits and other essential figures on the chart.
b. Plot the means on the chart.

17-2. An automatic machine produces 5.0 millimeter bolts at a high rate of speed. A quality-control program has been started to control the number of defectives. The quality-control inspector selects 50 bolts at random and determines how many are defective. the numbers defective for the first 10 samples are 3, 5, 0, 4, 1, 2, 6, 5, 7, and 7. (Textbook Problem 17-25)

a. Design a percent defective chart. Insert $\bar{p}$, LCL, UCL and the percents defective on the chart.
b. Plot the number of defects for the first 10 samples on the chart.
c. Interpret the chart.

CHAPTER
18
TIME SERIES AND FORECASTING

CHAPTER GOALS

After completing this chapter, you will be able to:

1. Explain the meaning of each component of a time series.

2. Use Excel to determine and display the linear trend equation.

3. Use Excel and linear trend equations to arrive at and display estimates for future time periods.

Introduction

In Chapter 13, Regression and Correlation, we used the topic of regression analysis as a tool for model building and prediction. The emphasis in this chapter of time series analysis and forecasting is similar because, like in Chapter 13, we will focus only on linear data. However, now we will expand the concept by forecasting future events.

Although numerous forecasting methods have been devised, they all have one common goal, to predict future events. Projections can then be incorporated into the decision-making process. The only quantitative forecasting method studied in this chapter uses a simple straight line regression equation. Perhaps because of its simplicity and lack of sophistication, time series analysis is still a popular technique in forecasting the future. Historical data and past happenings are studied to better understand the underlying structure of the data and, if the data fits a linear model, we simply extend these past trends into the future. A scatter diagram is often useful to visualize the appropriateness of linear forecasting.

The long-term trends of many business series, such as sales, exports, and production, often approximate a straight line. If so, the equation to describe this growth is: $Y' = a + bt$, where:

Y' read Y prime, is the projected value of the Y variable for a selected value of t.

a   is the Y-intercept, it is the estimated value of Y when $t = 0$. Another way to put it is the estimated value of Y where the straight line crosses the Y-axis when t is 0

b   is the slope of the line, or the average change in Y' for each change of one unit (either increase or decrease) in t.

t   is any value of time selected.

Plotting a Trendline

In Chapter 13 you used Excel's ChartWizard function to construct a scatterplot, then inserted a linear trendline, obtaining a linear equation. You will use the same procedure in this chapter.

Example 1. Annual production of king-size rockers by Wood Products, Inc. since 1993 follows:

Year	Production (thousands)
1996	4
1997	8
1998	5
1999	8
2000	11
2001	9
2002	11
2003	14

a. Plot the production data.

b. Determine the least squares equation.

c. Based on the equation for the straight line, what is the estimated production for 2006?

d. For 2015?

1. On a new worksheet enter the data as follows.

	A	B	C
1	Actual Yr	Year Num	Production
2	1996	1	4
3	1997	2	8
4	1998	3	5
5	1999	4	8
6	2000	5	11
7	2001	6	9
8	2002	7	11
9	2003	8	14

The years need to be in sequence starting with year 1.

2. Highlight **B1:C9**. From the Menu bar select ChartWizard.

3. In Step 1, under Chart type, select XY (Scatter). Under Chart sub-type, the upper left chart should be selected. Click Next.

4. In Step 2, accept the defaults. Click Next.

5. In Step 3, at the top, the Titles tab should be selected. Click on the Chart Tiltle text box, key **Annual Production: Wood Products Inc.** Tab to the Value (X) axis text box. Key **Year.** Tab to the Value (Y) axis text box. Key **Production (thousands)**

6. At the top, select the Legend tab. Click in the Show legend check box to de-select the legend. Click Finish.

A condensed chart appears

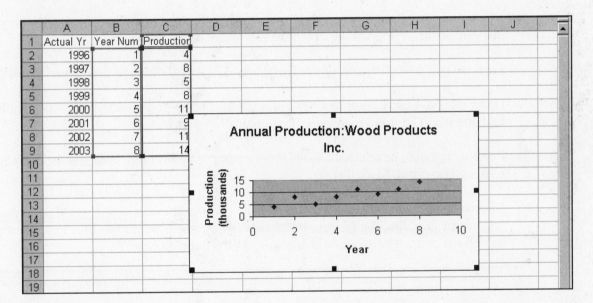

7. With the handles still on the chart, click and hold the left mouse button inside the chart. A 4-way arrow will show in the chart. As you move the chart it will show as an open box with dashed lines. With your mouse button still depressed, drag your mouse and move your chart so the left edge of the chart is in column D and the top edge of the chart is in row 1.

8. Click on the bottom handle of the chart. Drag the bottom lime to row 17.

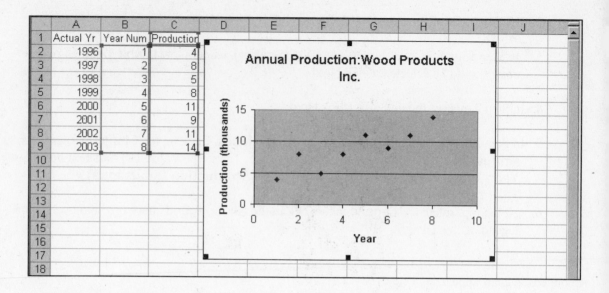

9. Make sure the handles show on the chart box. With your **right** mouse arrow, click on one of the data points. There will be a dot inserted in each data point.

10. From the pull down list, select Add Trendline. The Add Trendline dialog box appears.

11. Under the Type tab, Linear should be selected for Trend/Regression type. Click on the Options tab. The Add Trendline Options dialog box appears.

12. Automatic should be selected under Trendline name. Select the check box for Display equation on chart. Click Ok.

13. Click on the equation. A shadow box appears. Place your mouse arrow on the upper line between two handles. Make sure your mouse arrow remains an arrow. Move the equation box off the chart. The trendline is displayed with the equation for Y'.

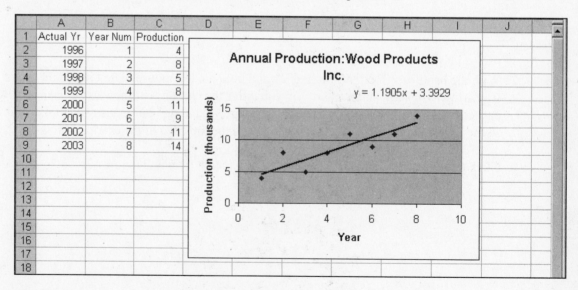

You can use the trendline chart and the equation to make projections into the future.

Chapter 18

Example 1, part c. What is the estimated production for 2006?

1. Make sure the handles are on your chart. Click your **right** mouse arrow on the trendline. Select Format Trendline. Select the Options tab. Under Forecast, key **3** in the Forward text box or click on the up arrow of the scroll bar until the number 3 is displayed in the text box. Click OK.

The number 3 was used for the forecast number because the last known year was 2003 and 2006 is three years into the future.

2. In A10:B10 type, **2006** and **11** respectively.

You will use the equation for Y' to compute the projection for the year 2006. It is the 11th year in the sequence. The formula is $Y' = a + bt$. This equation is displayed on the chart as y = 1.1905x + 3.3929, where 3.3929 is the value of a, 1.1905 is the value of b, and x is used instead of t.

3. In C10 type, **=3.3929+1.1905*B10**

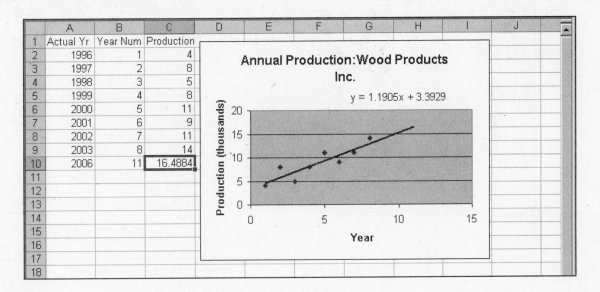

From the chart you can see that the projected trendline for the 11th year is a little above 15 on the Y axis. This is confirmed by computing the value of Y' for the 11th year which is 16.4884.

Example 1, part d. What is the estimated production for 2015?

1. Make sure the handles are on your chart. Click your **right** mouse arrow on the trendline. Select F̲ormat T̲rendline. Select the Options tab. Under Forecast, key **12** in the F̲oreward text box or click on the up arrow of the scroll bar until the number 12 is displayed in the text box. Click OK.

The number 12 was used for the forecast number because the last known year was 2003 and 2015 is twelve years into the future.

2. In A11:B11 type, **2015** and **20** respectively.

You will use the same equation for Y' to compute the projection for the year 2015. It is the 20th year in the sequence.

3. Drag the lower right handle of C10 to C11 to copy the formula.

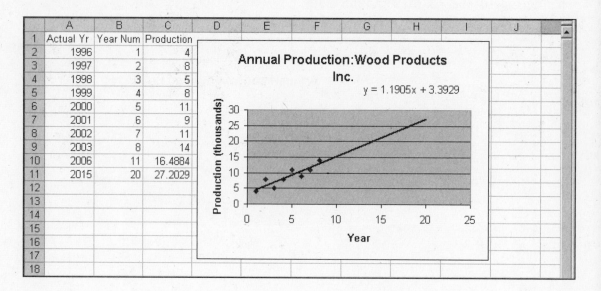

From the chart you can see that the projected trendline for the 20th year is a little above 25 on the Y axis. This is confirmed by computing the value of Y' for the 20th year which is 27.2029.

If you wish save your file as **projt-1**. Close your file.

Practice Exercises taken from textbook.

18-1. The sales, in billions of dollars, of Keller Overhead Door, Inc, for 1998 to 2003 are:
Textbook Problem 19-18).

Year	Sales
1998	7.45
1999	7.83
2000	8.07
2001	7.94
2002	7.76
2003	7.90

a. Use Excel to plot the data.
b. Use Excel to determine the least squares trend equation, and provide a trendline.
c. Estimate the net sales for the year 2006.
d. Estimate the net sales for 2013.

18-2. Listed below is the selling price for a share of PepsiCo, Inc., at the close of the year.: (Textbook Problem 19-20)

Year	Price
1990	12.9135
1991	16.8250
1992	20.6125
1993	20.3024
1994	18.3160
1995	27.7538
1996	29.0581
1997	36.0155
1998	40.6111
1999	35.0230
2000	49.5625
2001	48.6800
2002	42.2200

a. Use Excel to plot the data.
b. Use Excel to determine the least square trendline equation, and provide a trendlime.
c. Estimate the selling price in 2005.
d. Estimate the selling price in 2020.

McGRAW-HILL/Irwin

Basic Statistics Using Excel for Office XP for use with STATISTICAL TECHNIQUES IN BUSINESS & ECONOMICS, Twelfth Edition by Lind, Marchal and Wathen.

We hope this manual and the text are error free and easy for you to use. Invariably, however, if there are errors, we would appreciate knowing about such errors as soon as possible so that we can correct them in subsequent printings and future editions. Please help us by using this postage-paid form to report any that you find. Thank you.

Note: Extra copies of this form appear at the end of this manual.
Attention: R. T. Hercher

Name _____   School _____

Office Phone _____

Please fold and seal so that our address is visible.

BUSINESS REPLY MAIL

FIRST-CLASS MAIL   PERMIT NO.204   OAKBROOK, IL

POSTAGE WILL BE PAID BY ADDRESSEE

ATTENTION: R. T. Hercher

THE McGRAW-HILL COMPANIES
1333 BURR RIDGE PKY.
BURR RIDGE, IL 60527-0085

(fold)

(fold)

McGRAW-HILL/Irwin

Basic Statistics Using Excel[☐] for Office XP[☐] for use with STATISTICAL TECHNIQUES IN BUSINESS & ECONOMICS, Twelfth Edition by Lind, Marchal and Wathen.

We hope this manual and the text are error free and easy for you to use. Invariably, however, if there are errors, we would appreciate knowing about such errors as soon as possible so that we can correct them in subsequent printings and future editions. Please help us by using this postage-paid form to report any that you find. Thank you.

Note: Extra copies of this form appear at the end of this manual.
Attention: R. T. Hercher

Name _____   School _____

Office Phone _____

Please fold and seal so that our address is visible.

BUSINESS REPLY MAIL
FIRST-CLASS MAIL   PERMIT NO.204   OAKBROOK, IL

POSTAGE WILL BE PAID BY ADDRESSEE

ATTENTION: R. T. Hercher

THE McGRAW-HILL COMPANIES
1333 BURR RIDGE PKY.
BURR RIDGE, IL 60527-0085

(fold)

(fold)